Mary Wollstonecraft: writer

WITHDRAWN

Mary Wollstonecraft: Writer

Harriet Devine Jump

Lecturer in English
Edge Hill College

 HARVESTER
WHEATSHEAF

New York   London   Toronto   Sydney   Tokyo   Singapore

First published 1994 by
Harvester Wheatsheaf
Campus 400, Maylands Avenue
Hemel Hempstead
Hertfordshire, HP2 7EZ
A division of
Simon & Schuster International Group

Typeset in 10/12pt Plantin
by Hands Fotoset, Leicester

Printed and bound in Great Britain by
Biddles Ltd, Guildford and King's Lynn

British Library Cataloguing in Publication Data

A catalogue record for this book is available from
the British Library

ISBN 0-7450-0784-8

1 2 3 4 5   98 97 96 95 94

For William, Sophie and Oliver

Those who are bold enough to advance before the age they live in, and to throw off, by the force of their own minds, the prejudices which the maturing reason of the world will in time disavow, must learn to brave censure. We ought not to be too anxious respecting the opinion of others.
(Mary Wollstonecraft to Mary Hays, *c.* summer 1797)

Contents

Chapter 6

Chapter 7

Chapter 8

Appendix

Preface

I first encountered Mary Wollstonecraft's writings when I was a postgraduate student. I was struck at once, as most people who read her books are struck, with the freshness and immediacy of her approach. But it was not until a few years later, when I was asked to lecture on her writings to undergraduates on the Women's Writing course at Oxford University, that I came to appreciate the range and variety of her literary output, and to see how important her work was to the history of ideas of her period. I also realised that although there were biographies, and a limited number of good articles on her work, there was at the time no full-length study of her writing and thought to which students could refer. The present work owes its existence to that realisation.

The recent revival of interest in Wollstonecraft's writings owes much to the emergence of feminist literary studies. Her *Vindication of the Rights of Woman* (1792) was rescued from relative obscurity in the 1960s and hailed as a classic text for feminism, and her two novels have also been interpreted in the context of women's writing. Considerable emphasis has been placed on the more sombre elements of her biography, but until recently critics have paid little attention to the rest of her literary output.

The past few years have seen a proliferation of works by and about Wollstonecraft: editions, both individual and collected; anthologies; biographies; criticism – even a novel based on her life. Some of the best writing, not surprisingly, has been by feminist critics. Possibly the most admired modern study is Mary Poovey's *The Proper Lady and the Woman Writer: Ideology as Style in the Works of Mary Wollstonecraft, Mary Shelley and Jane Austen* (1984). Poovey assumes that there is a specifically masculine and feminine rhetoric, and that Wollstonecraft's reply to Burke failed, ultimately, because she 'retreats into the masculine literary conventions whose artifice she claims to despise' (Poovey (1984) p. 68). She pictures Wollstonecraft trapped within the very ideology she was striving to alter. Cora Kaplan's essays (1985, 1986) interpret Wollstonecraft's writings in the light of socialist feminist criticism; while those of Mitzi Myers reconsider the whole body of her work, and attempt to place it within its historical and cultural context. More recently, Tom Furniss (1991) and Vivien Jones (1992) have both written interestingly on the relation between gender and style in her political writings; and Jane Moore (1992) has applied Lacanian critical theory to Wollstonecraft's *Letters from Sweden*.

On the whole, Wollstonecraft has been less well served by biographies and more general studies of her texts. The best-known biography, by Claire Tomalin (1977), suggests that its author dislikes her subject; while Janet Todd, a pioneering editor and critic of Wollstonecraft's writings, recently described her as 'a repetitive writer', and judged that 'it is possible to come from much of her writing with a sense of frustration' (Todd (1990) p. [ix]). Jennifer Lorch's *Mary Wollstonecraft: The Making of a Radical Feminist* (1990), while it uncovers no new material, makes intelligent observations about her writings.

The most impressive recent full-length study must be Gary Kelly's *Revolutionary Feminism* (1992). He takes her work as a whole with absolute seriousness, and argues for a view of both her ideas and her writing style as a response to the cultural revolution which was taking place in Britain during the late eighteenth century. In particular, he places her work in the context of the Revolutionary crisis of the 1790s, and sees her as aiming to re-revolutionise the cultural construction of 'woman'. Nevertheless, like other commentators on Wollstonecraft, he overlooks the ways in which her thinking changed and developed towards the end of her writing life. Like other English radicals whose enthusiasm for 'Revolution principles' took them to France to view events at first hand, Wollstonecraft found herself in a dilemma when she was confronted with events such as the arrests and executions of some of her friends and acquaintances, and the blood bath of the

Terror; and her writings from this period demonstrate the widening gap between the optimism of her theories and the pessimism born of her observation of the realities. Her struggles to close this gap are revealed by an attentive reading of these works. Also, although Kelly suggests that in her later writings Wollstonecraft 'prefigured' Wordsworth and the Romantics, he does not develop this important idea in any detail.

While it acknowledges the difficulty of seeing beyond the undeniable fact that Wollstonecraft as woman has become a twentieth-century icon, the present work attempts to situate her more firmly in the context of her own time. In particular, her connections and affinities with her contemporaries – especially those generally thought of as Romantics – have been emphasised. As a writer, Wollstonecraft began in the tradition of eighteenth-century Enlightenment, but the events of her life, the influential friendships she made and, above all, her willingness to review her own thinking in the light of experience, give her more in common with the writers of the Romantic period than has previously been acknowledged.

Mary Wollstonecraft: Writer aims at a survey of all Wollstonecraft's writings, in the hope of correcting some of those extreme emphases which have been placed on the feminist aspects of her work. Her importance as a theorist on the position of women in society is undeniable, but she was also concerned with wider social, educational and aesthetic issues. By including discussion of her earliest educational works (*Thoughts on the Education of Daughters* and *Original Stories from Real Life*), her reviews for the *Analytical*, her books on the French Revolution (*A Vindication of the Rights of Men* and *An Historical and Moral View of . . . The French Revolution*) and her later non-fictional writings, *Letters from Sweden* and the Essay on Poetry, this book hopes to demonstrate her centrality in the history of ideas of her period.

In addition to offering an introduction to the whole body of Wollstonecraft's work, *Mary Wollstonecraft: Writer* hopes to show the relevance not so much of her biography (which is widely available elsewhere) as of what might be called her psychobiography. 'We reason deeply, when we forcibly feel', she wrote in the *Letters from Sweden*, and it can be seen that some of the most interesting features of her writing resulted from the painful emotional experiences of her life. This book argues that her unrequited love for Henry Fuseli may have produced the sometimes harsh, always ambivalent treatment of female sexuality in the *Rights of Woman* which has been a much-debated topic among Wollstonecraft's critics. Later chapters discuss the contradictions and ambivalences of the *Historical and Moral View*, and trace the effects of rejection as they emerge in her writing after she was deserted by Gilbert Imlay.

The aim of the book is to provide an introduction to the work of Wollstonecraft for the general reader. Specialists are well catered for already. Undergraduate students, especially those studying English literature, history, cultural or women's studies, will welcome, I hope, a book which places Wollstonecraft in the context of her life and her times. A short list of further reading has been added; this should be useful to those who wish to follow up this study in more detail, or to place it more exactly in the framework of its age.

I would like to thank Edge Hill College of Higher Education for their encouragement in awarding me a research grant to help me to complete this book. I am grateful to Brian Maidment, John Simons and Gill Davies for their support and encouragement.

My thanks to the library staff at the Bodleian Library, Oxford, and to Edge Hill College Library. A version of part of Chapter 5 appeared in 'The Cool Eye of Observation: Mary Wollstonecraft and the French Revolution', in Kelvin Everest (ed.), *Revolution in Writing: British Literary Responses to the French Revolution* (Milton Keynes, 1991). A version of part of Chapters 6 and 8 appeared in 'No Equal Mind: Mary Wollstonecraft and the Young Romantics', *Charles Lamb Bulletin*, New Series, no. 79 (July 1992): 225–38. I am grateful to the editor for permission to reprint.

My greatest debt of gratitude is to Alun R. Jones, without whose help and support this book would not have been completed.

◆

Chapter I

Thoughts on the Education of Daughters (1787)
Mary: A Fiction (1788)
Original Stories from Real Life (1788)
Lessons (1798)

Mary Wollstonecraft is properly celebrated for her feminism and her radicalism, but the works which form the subject of this chapter were all composed before she became either a feminist or a radical, and they are no less interesting for that. As a writer she was a late starter – she was 28 years old when her first book was published – and while these first publications, being her first attempts in a variety of forms, may have little intrinsic merit, they cannnot be ignored, since they show clearly the speed, courage and skill with which she developed. Indeed, her development cannot be discussed without taking them into account, since they also demonstrate the ways in which her emerging radicalism brought into question the orthodoxy of her early beliefs and the conventional assumptions of her upbringing. In particular, she moved in four or five years from resignation and acceptance to rejection and revolt. She still clung to some kind of Rousseauesque Deism, but was no longer willing to accept that social deprivation and misery constituted a necessary preparation for either character formation or entry into the Christian heaven.

With the exception of her translations – a fairly painless way of making money, but also an education in themselves: she found herself, and her voice, largely by translating other people's works – all the works she produced during these early years were on the subject of education. This is not surprising, since her first attempt at a career – apart from an unsatisfactory stint as a lady's companion – was as a teacher in her own school. According to her husband William Godwin:

I

No person was ever better formed for the business of education. . . .
With children she was the mirror of patience. Perhaps, in all her
extensive experience upon the subject of education, she never betrayed
one symptom of irascibility. . . . Another eminent advantage she
possessed in the business of education, was that she was little troubled
with scepticism and uncertainty. She saw, as it were by intuition, the
path which her mind determined to pursue, and had a firm confidence
in her power to effect what she desired. (Holmes (1987) pp. 218–19)

She interrupted her teaching in autumn 1785 to go to Lisbon to
attend her friend Fanny Blood's lying-in. She arrived to find her
already in labour; thus she was present, a few days afterwards, at her
death – which tragically foreshadowed her own death following the
birth of her daughter twelve years later. In February 1786 she
returned from Lisbon to find that 'the school had suffered
considerably in her absence' (Holmes (1987) p. 220), and that Fanny's
family were in financial difficulties. Within six weeks she had written
*Thoughts on the Education of Daughters: with Reflections on Female
Conduct in the more important Duties of Life*, which her friend John
Hewlett helped her to sell to the radical publisher Joseph Johnson for
10 guineas, some of which she used to send Mr and Mrs Blood to
Dublin (Wardle (1979) p. 105). Johnson published *The Education of
Daughters* in January 1787.

Wollstonecraft seems to have had the journalist's gift – or vice – of
working best rapidly and under pressure to meet a deadline or pay
off a debt: perhaps such conditions stimulated the energy and
application she needed in order to compose. This work, however, has
the signs of haste and carelessness everywhere – it is jumbled, at times
to the point of incoherence. There is little, if anything, in the way of
consistent argument or point of view, merely a *mélange* of opinions
and observations. Nevertheless, it does provide a useful demonstration of the direction her thinking was taking.

As its full title indicates, *The Education of Daughters* combines two
genres which were becoming increasingly popular at the end of the
eighteenth century: conduct books and works on female education.
As a teacher, Wollstonecraft had a practical interest in educational
theory, and she quotes from the work which had had a decisive
influence on subsequent writers on the subject, John Locke's *Some
Thoughts Concerning Education* (1693). Locke's emphasis on good
example, learning through pleasure rather than rote, and sympathy
and tolerance, as well as his stated goal of the development of virtue,

wisdom and a liberal spirit, were repeated with variations throughout the eighteenth century. Locke's principal aim had been the education of boys, but the last quarter of the century saw a proliferation of works on female education written by both men and women. Education for girls was a matter of cultivating the virtues that society considered feminine: compassion, charity, truthfulness, and government of the temper. Rarely was equality of education for the sexes suggested. On the contrary, male and female writers alike stressed the undesirability of a woman being overeducated: educated, in other words, to the point where her intelligence and knowledge would be seen as threatening to male society. Hester Chapone, for example, wrote in her *Letters on the Improvement of the Mind, Addressed to a Young Lady* (2 vols, 1773):

> The danger of pedantry and presumption in a woman – of her exciting envy in one sex and jealousy in the other – of her exchanging the graces of imagination for the severity and preciseness of a scholar, would be, I own, sufficient to frighten me from the ambition of seeing my girl remarkable for learning. (ii, p. 121)

In addition, much emphasis was placed on the desirability of acquiring the virtue of Christian resignation, which Wollstonecraft also recommended in her work (iv, pp. 108–10). Hannah More, in *Essays on Various Subjects, Principally Designed for Young Ladies* (1777), argued that a bold, enterprising spirit, admired in boys, must be suppressed in girls, who needed to develop a 'submissive temper and a forbearing spirit' (p. 145). In her view, 'A girl who has docility will seldom be found to want understanding enough for all the purposes of a social, a happy, and a useful life' (p. 149). John Moir, in his *Female Tuition: or, An Address to Mothers* (1784), recommended that women 'should be accustomed to the earliest habits of subjection and obedience . . . it [does not] seem the intention of nature, they should openly at least assume the lead' (p. 7). He suggested that the best way to do this was to make them comfortable at home and 'rivet their young and ardent attentions wholly on domestic concerns' (p. 44). Most writers were, however, agreed on the desirability of a certain amount of 'adornment' of the mind, in order that a woman could be 'capable of becoming a conversable companion to her husband', as Vicesimus Knox put it in his *Essays Moral and Literary* (1779).[1] Even Vicesimus Knox's fictional clergyman's daughter, who has been given a 'male' education by her father, is careful to add that she 'did not neglect the ornamental accomplishments' of music, dancing and attention to dress – especially important, since lack of 'accurate cleanliness . . . sometimes involved literary ladies in deserved disgrace' (Jones (1990) p. 108). Knox's essay is unusual, of its kind, in arguing:

> That learning belongs not to the female character, and that the female mind is not capable of a degree of improvement equal to that of the other sex, are narrow and unphilosophical prejudices. (Jones (1990) p. 109)

Even so, it displays a profound ambivalence about the desirability of becoming a learned woman, and the clergyman's daughter writes that she regrets the fact that the gentlemen avoid her because they 'entertain a notion, that a lady of improved understanding will not submit to the less dignified cares of managing a household' (*ibid.*).

In *The Education of Daughters* Wollstonecraft acknowledges her familiarity with existing educational theories, although she expresses doubts about their practical applicability, since to be able to follow them 'the parents must have subdued their own passions, which is not often the case in any considerable degree' (iv, p. 9). She also had her own practical experience of teaching on which to draw. But little information can be gleaned from *The Education of Daughters* about the day-to-day running of Wollstonecraft's school in Newington Green, which, although it must have influenced her decision to write on female education, provides little or no background material. Indeed, Wollstonecraft states that the best education is to be had at home, since boarding schools teach badly, cultivate follies, and overemphasise accomplishments at the expense of solid virtues (iv, p. 22): all these points would be made later, and more forcibly, in the *Rights of Woman*. A parent who bought the work hoping for some practical advice about what subjects to teach or which books to buy would have been severely disappointed. One chapter recommends the development of taste, through the practice of music and drawing, and states that, in writing, style should be given attention – her own style and grammar are, as demonstrated, rather shaky – and that reading should be used to fill time and add knowledge (iv, pp. 18–19). A further chapter on reading ('the most rational employment. . . . Judicious books enlarge the mind' (iv, p. 20)) speaks out forcibly against the reading of novels, which place too much emphasis on sensibility and the passions, and recommends books which blend instruction and amusement: Johnson's *The Adventurer* has the distinction of being the only work – apart from the Bible – actually to be mentioned by name (iv, pp. 20–1).

This lack of practical advice should not be seen as a flaw. Step-by-step recommendations were never of great concern to Wollstonecraft: this is as true of her later, more polemical, works as it is of *The Education of Daughters*, which, in any case, she offers merely as *Thoughts* of a philosophical kind, mixed with some practical advice. For her, education was primarily a training in morality. She was a firm believer in the idea that if what she came to call 'first principles' were properly established, the details would take care of themselves. In this work as much as in any of her later writings, it is the manner in which the mind is formed and developed which is her overriding concern. A child, she believes, is born with instincts and passions which it is the business of education to bring under the control of reason. She held it to be 'a well-proved fact':

> that principles of truth are innate. Without reasoning, we assent to many truths; we feel their force, and artful sophistry can only blunt those feelings which nature has implanted in us as instinctive guides to virtue. (iv, p. 9)

Since children also have an innate capacity for reason, it is the business of the parents to develop that capacity as much as possible. This is to be achieved by constant attention to mental development. Questions must always be given reasonable answers; children must be preserved from 'receiving wrong impressions'; above all, they must, if possible, be taught to 'combine their ideas. . . . I wish them to be taught to think' (iv, pp. 10–11). But the development of the ability to reason, however desirable, is not an end in itself. 'The main business of our lives is to learn to be virtuous' (iv, p. 27), and intellectual development, by helping 'to make a person in some measure independent of the senses, is a prop to virtue' (iv, p. 12). In addition, constant attention must be paid to learning to control the temper, and to the development of gentleness and humility, which are not innate but require cultivation. These qualities must, however, be the result of good sense rather than weakness – in a passage which anticipates the radicalism of her later works, Wollstonecraft asserts that: 'She who submits, without conviction, to a parent or husband, will as unreasonably tyrannize over her servants; for slavish fear and tyranny go together' (iv, p. 23). This short passage, incidentally, shows Wollstonecraft writing at her best, in an anticipation of her later style. It is rare at this stage in her development: almost aphoristic, pithily turned and carrying immediate conviction, it has made its point almost before it can be questioned.

Thus far – about halfway through the work – Wollstonecraft has addressed herself to the subject of education. Although the emphasis she places on the psychology of the learning process is more strongly marked than in comparable works of the period, the ideas are clearly derived from a number of identifiable sources – chiefly Locke's influential treatise, combined with her friend and mentor Richard Price's moral philosophy[2] – and the attitudes to women's roles and duties is little different from that of other contemporary women writers.

The Education of Daughters is not logically structured or organised, but there seems to be some attempt at a division into two halves, although this is not marked specifically at any point. After her essay on 'Boarding Schools', the essays broaden in scope to encompass the subject proposed in the second part of her full title, 'Reflections on Female Conduct in the more important Duties of Life'. For many readers, this has appeared the livelier part of her book. Wollstone-craft, throughout her writing life, is at her most convincing when she is able to draw on her own experiences and observations: indeed, this becomes one of the strongest features of her style and arguments.

There is nothing in any of the contemporary educational works or conduct books which resembles Wollstonecraft's chapter on 'The Unfortunate Situation of Females, fashionably educated, and left without a fortune'. This is partly owing, no doubt, to the fact that she was able to identify with (at least) the second part of this chapter title: it is impossible to mistake the deep personal feeling which lies behind the statement – again, vintage Wollstonecraft in its aphoristic bitterness – that 'Few are the modes of earning a subsistence, and those are very humiliating' (iv, p. 25). As always, however, her involvement leads her to think beyond her own individual situation, though as always it is her poverty, her humiliation, her sense of neglect that form the basis of her arguments. The result is her first attempt at a criticism of women's experience of the social conditions of the marketplace. The disadvantages of work as a companion, a teacher, or a governess are described with a withering brevity, and Wollstonecraft regrets that the trades have ceased to be respectable since they fell into the hands of men. She ends the chapter with a survey of the grave disadvantages inherent in the position of an attractive woman without financial means: once again, there is little doubt that she is writing from her own personal experience. A woman in this position, she writes, is in constant danger of seduction, and it is rare for her to be able to marry, a situation which frequently leads to severe disappointment. Although her thinking has some way to go on these issues – the only solution she is able to offer is Christian resignation – it is clear that her dissatisfaction with the opportunities open to women is already taking shape.

In the chapter on 'Love', she confesses that 'there is not a subject that admits so little of reasoning' (iv, p. 28). Although she advocates the exertion of reason over passion ('I am very far from thinking love irresistible, and not to be conquered' (iv, p. 29)), this sternly advocated stoicism is undermined by the fact that she has already admitted that anyone who is in a position to consider the matter will already be seeing 'through the medium of passion', so that 'its suggestions are mistaken for those of reason' (iv, p. 28). Despite the difficulties, however, the subject draws her into a discussion of several issues which are related to the inequalities of women's position in society. One is the problem of 'male coquets', whose vanity leads them to make conquests with no intention of marrying: they are, she argues, more pernicious than the female kind, because 'their sphere of action is larger, and they are less exposed to the censure of the world' (*ibid.*). Almost certainly she was thinking of a recent experience of her own: her encounter in Bath with the young Cambridge don Joshua Waterhouse, who seems to have led her on without any intention of marrying her. She points out that women are not in a position to complain about such behaviour, and describes the misery, 'for a delicate mind', of loving someone of whom the reason disapproves. Although this is not solely a female problem, she argues the point from a woman's perspective, advocating a marriage of esteem, even without love if necessary, as more conducive to peace of mind (iv, p. 29). She warns against 'platonic attachments': a woman's heart is 'very treacherous', and too easily betrayed into 'sighing for impossibilities'. Once again, she is unable to suggest a solution apart from that of 'the calm satisfaction which resignation produces' (iv, p. 30).

The relationship between submission and tyranny on which she touched earlier in the work is not discussed in the chapter on 'Matrimony'. She is concerned instead with the intellectual and moral development of women, which, she argues, will be arrested by an early marriage. She is conscious of the advantage which men have over women: their activities in the world are such that their intellectual faculties will be developed, and they have to get to know the world in order to function in it successfully. Women, on the other hand, too often allow their reason to lie dormant:

> Nothing, I am sure, calls forth the faculties so much as the being obliged to struggle with the world; and this is not a woman's province in the married state. Her sphere of action is not large, and if she is not taught to look into her own heart, how trivial are her occupations and pursuits! What little arts engross and narrow her mind! (iv, p. 32)

Even if her marriage is happy, a woman will be more contented if she possesses a cultivated mind. The development of the intellect is of even greater importance for a 'sensible delicate woman, who by some strange accident is joined to a fool or a brute'; she will be 'wretched beyond all names of wretchedness' unless she has managed to develop her capacities to some extent (iv, pp. 32–3). But Wollstonecraft is not arguing against marriage as an institution: behind the whole work is the obvious and agreed assumption that the education of daughters is an education for a good marriage. This is the actual subject, the hidden agenda, behind the whole work. She is instructing mothers how to raise daughters to be valuable commodities in the marriage market, where, after all, they must make the best career they can by marrying well. It is their duty to serve God and society as best they can in the sphere of activity necessarily limited by their domestic obligations. While she is clearly questioning the status quo, and worrying at it, she none the less accepts the establishment view with little or no modification – at best one can notice the occasional restlessness in her thinking.

The Education of Daughters ends with a series of essays which have abandoned any pretence at organisation – one is actually called 'Desultory Thoughts'. A strong Calvinism runs through much of what she says: she condemns the triviality of card-playing, for example, because it teaches the vices of avarice to both young and old, and feeds idleness and ignorance; worries about the purity and happiness of the young being a prey to vice and folly in 'Public Places', and takes a puritanical attitude to dress, which should be plain. She has the puritan's sense of seriousness and distrust of levity and frivolity (there has always, of course, been a strong link between puritanism and radicalism). Reason, purity and virtue are felt to be serious matters – there is a sense that if a virtuous and reasonable young lady is not happy, then she can only have herself to blame. In 'The Benefits which arise from Disappointments' she argues the well-worn Stoic case of the benefits and pleasures to be derived from adversity in an orgy of wishful thinking in which she turns all her miseries into virtues and all her pleasures into vices. Sympathy for one's fellows learnt through misery is a lesson she herself is beginning to take in, though she overlooks the pain and suffering (obvious from her letters at the time) which is the price to be paid for this particular lesson. In the end she cannot satisfactorily handle the problems she raises, and falls back on the conventional solutions of reason and benevolence, and the old religious solution to problems human and social: 'our finding things unsatisfactory here, should force us to think of the better country to which we are going' (iv, p. 37) – Christianity as the religion of slaves, used by the governors to keep them in their place. She has not followed through her arguments, though all the material is in place for a radical social critique. Later, on the basis of similar – identical, perhaps – material, she builds an argument to undermine the status quo. Here, she reinforces it while asking awkward questions, mainly of herself.

It is easy to be critical of the work's failings, but this is, after all, 'prentice work, and should not be taken too seriously. Wollstonecraft is as concerned to find a 'tone' and an 'attitude', and the correct rhetorical conventions – to find, in other words, a solidarity and consensus with an existing audience – as she is with what she has to say. She is concerned with selling the book more than with selling her views; indeed, at this stage she is not at all sure what her views are: they often seem to surprise her as she articulates them, and hence give rise to a good deal of contradiction. She has undoubtedly, to an outstanding degree, the ability to turn her own experience into generalities, to abstract from the particular; though at this stage her experiences, acute and painful as they were, were also restricted and narrow. She was only gradually becoming aware of the extent to which, as a person and as a woman, she had been conditioned by her society and environment; and she had not even begun, in any real

sense, to break free. She had, however, begun to become aware of the
situation, and to generalise on the basis of her analysis of it: the book
is a most interesting demonstration of Wollstonecraft beginning to
construct herself as a prototype woman. But she still reinforces
society, environment and conventional attitudes while arguing for a
more enlightened, more reasonable approach to the question of
women and womanhood.

Apart from a favourable mention in *The Monthly Review*, *The
Education of Daughters* was not noticed by the reviewers despite its
incipient radicalism. But the fact that she was now a published author
must have given Wollstonecraft some confidence in her own abilities;
and writing the book had brought her into contact with Joseph
Johnson, who was to exert such a decisive influence over the course
of her future life and career.

After the didacticism of *The Education of Daughters*, Wollstonecraft
experimented next with fiction. Her determination to master both
forms clearly shows that she had decided her future was not in
teaching or as a governess but in the world of writing, of ideas, with
the possibility of influencing events. In this a woman had at least an
outside chance of competing with men on terms which were far from
equal but none the less acceptable when all the alternatives were
considered.

Mary was written in the late summer of 1787, while Wollstonecraft
was employed as a governess to the daughters of Lord and Lady
Kingsborough, at Mitchelstown Castle in Ireland – the exact date of
composition is not certain, but the book was finished by September
(Wardle (1979) p. 162). Her letters during the first six months of the
year provide an unusually full list of works which she was reading at
the time. Wishing to improve her French, she undertook in January
to read some novels in that language, including Madame de Genlis's
Les Veillés du Château and Baroness de Montolière's *Caroline de
Litchfield* (Wardle (1979) pp. 132–3). Two months later she was
reading Rousseau's *Émile* in French. Although *Émile* is heavily
criticised for its anti-feminism in *The Rights of Woman*, Wollstonecraft seems not to have been troubled by this in 1787. In any case,
she was always able to find a great deal to admire in Rousseau's
writings, and she explicitly identifies with him in a letter of March
1787: 'he rambles into that *chimerical* world in which I too have often
wandered' (Wardle (1979) p. 145).

It is clear that his 'collection of scattered thoughts and observations

[with] little continuity' (Rousseau (1974) p. 1) was strongly influential on both the style and content of *Mary*. Rousseau emphasised the benefits of a simple, rural existence, away from the corrupting effects of contemporary society, arguing that vice and error are alien to man's constitution. Growing up in a natural environment, the child will develop the innate goodness in his own nature, learning to control the passions, which are in themselves neither good nor bad, taking on those qualities in proportion as we control or are controlled by them. It is, in fact, the feelings which Rousseau sees as impelling our development. As the child matures, he will grow in sensibility, reason and imagination, all of which fit him for a full interaction with the world of nature and of human relations. Sensibility, in particular, is the faculty which, through a response to the beauties of nature, leads the mind to a conviction of union with the divine order which underlies the outer material or physical world. In many respects *Mary* is an attempt at a feminist revision of Rousseau's theories.

The author's Advertisement distinguishes the heroine's character from those of Clarissa, Lady Grandison, and Sophie, the heroine of *Émile*, and describes the work as an 'artless' tale concerning a 'thinking' woman. Comedies or tragedies of manners and artifice seem to Wollstonecraft to be trivial, even objectionable, and in the first chapter the heroine's mother's addiction to the fashionable novels of sensibility – 'those delightful substitutes for bodily dissipation' (i, p. 8) – is treated with heavy irony. But these are the only models available to Wollstonecraft; she is obviously saturated in them, and falls back, none the less, on the very artifice she condemns.[3]

The story may be quickly told: the work is extremely brief, and becomes increasingly sparse as it progresses, suggesting that Wollstonecraft was in some haste to reach a conclusion. Mary, the sensitive, intelligent daughter of wealthy but unsatisfactory parents, manages to educate herself through reading and reflection, and develops into 'a woman, who has thinking powers' (i, p. 5). She enters into a friendship with the refined and delicate Ann – clearly based on Wollstonecraft's own relationship with Fanny Blood – but is disappointed to find that Ann's feelings do not match her own in intensity. By her mother's dying request she is married to a young man, who sets off on an extended tour of Europe without consummating the marriage. Mary accompanies the dying Ann to Lisbon in a fruitless search for health, and is befriended by an intelligent invalid, Henry, to whom she becomes increasingly attached. After Ann's death he promises to follow her to England, but his return is delayed by worsening sickness. When he finally appears, it is clear that he will not live long. His last weeks are spent in Mary's company, but her sense of duty to her absent and unloved husband prevents any union between them. He dies in her arms. She is unwillingly reunited with her husband, despite an extreme physical revulsion, and she is glad to detect symptoms of delicacy in her own health, as she believes she is 'hastening to that world *where there is neither marrying*, nor giving in marriage' (i, p. 73).

There are strong elements of emotional autobiography in this work: Wollstonecraft's feelings about the death of Fanny and her baby (probably a decisive emotional event); her resentment of the power and emptiness of privileged lives, in which she settles scores with Lady Kingsborough, and probably her mother as well, in one blow; her dreams of financial independence, from which freedom comes; her dreams – and dreads – of love with a man. But it will be clear that so far as the bare bones of the plot are concerned, there is not much to distinguish Wollstonecraft's fiction from a number of other contemporary works. Recent feminist critics have suggested that Mary's unwillingness to unite herself with a man whom she dislikes demonstrates a greater than usual fear of sexuality in the author (Spacks (1974–5) p. 139; Todd (1986) p. 123), but there seems little even here which could not be traced back, ultimately, to the enormously influential *Clarissa*. By deliberately adopting a narrative which reflects so many elements of the late-eighteenth-century novel, however, Wollstonecraft is clearly making an attempt to rewrite the genre. In other words, Mary's difference from other heroines should be most clearly demonstrable by the uniqueness of her reactions when she is faced with trials and tribulations which have become the stuff of fictional cliché.

This is an interesting and bold undertaking, but Wollstonecraft's lack of skill and experience prevents her from maintaining enough distance and objectivity to carry it through. *Mary* is not a success, but it is in many respects an admirable failure. It apparently sets out to deal with issues which had not been satisfactorily resolved in *The Education of Daughters*. While that work resolutely suggested – albeit with some hesitation – that feelings could be brought under the control of reason, *Mary* demonstrates the uncomfortable difficulties of achieving that end.

Wollstonecraft's debt to Rousseau becomes evident in a letter written shortly after the completion of *Mary*, in which she described the work as illustrative of 'an opinion of mine, that a genius will educate itself' (Wardle (1979) p. 162). This seems a curious opinion to be held by the recent author of a work on education; the more so since all Wollstonecraft's subsequent works place great emphasis on the importance of education in forming the mind. More than any of her other works, however, *Mary* attempts to accommodate and analyse the role of the unconscious, the instinctual and the innate. In *The Education of Daughters*, Wollstonecraft had expressed the opinion that 'the principles of truth are innate': that is to say, a child comes into the world already possessed of a feeling for 'truth', in addition to animal instincts and passions, and a capacity for reason. This idea is not developed in *The Education of Daughters*, although Wollstonecraft does state that this innate instinct can be repressed or stunted by incorrect education or associations. In *Mary* she explores this idea further: because she is forced by parental neglect to educate herself, Mary avoids the blunting effects of a poor education. Instead, her innate feeling for what Wollstonecraft appears to have regarded as the highest form of truth – the existence of 'the Great First Cause' (i, p. 11) – is allowed to develop fully and naturally through her sensitive appreciation of the beauties of nature and her compassion for her ailing mother. In addition, her reading of 'authors whose works were addressed to the understanding' (i, p. 19), her habit of considering and reflecting on everything she reads and observes, and her rigid self-control over her 'appetites and whims' (i, p. 17) all contribute to produce strength of mind and a habit of controlling (or sublimating) her frequently violent passions.

Although Mary's neglect by her family allows for the positive effects of self-education, it is not without its disadvantages. Her mother – a fine ironic portrait of a badly educated woman, self-absorbed, sickly and shallow – is singularly uninterested in her daughter, and laughs at the 'little secrets' which she confides. This has the unfortunate effect of turning Mary in on herself: reflection on her own feelings allows them to grow unnaturally strong, and she becomes 'too much the creature of impulse, and the slave of compassion' (i, p. 12). This seems to be intended as an example of a healthy instinct becoming perverted by wrong associations. Mary's 'sensibility' – a faculty defined by Wollstonecraft in an unfinished work of this period as 'the result of acute senses, finely fashioned nerves, which vibrate at the slightest touch, and convey such clear intelligence to the brain, that it does not require to be arranged by the judgement' (i, p. 201) – has led to her desire to love her fellow creatures, but her inability to develop that love through the normal channel of exchange with her mother allows it to acquire an almost neurotic strength and tenacity.

Mary's overdeveloped sensibility is possibly the most crucial issue in the work, and Wollstonecraft lacks the skill to explore it with sufficient clarity. Her account of Mary writing her 'rhapsody on sensibility' is given without irony or comment:

> Sensibility is the most exquisite feeling of which the human soul is susceptible: when it pervades us, we feel happy; and could it last unmixed, we might form some conjecture of the bliss of those paradisal days, when the obedient passions were under the dominion of reason, and the impulses of the heart did not need correction . . . it is this, which expands the soul, gives an enthusiastic greatness, mixed with tenderness, when we view the magnificent objects of nature; or hear of a good action. . . . Softened by tenderness, the soul is disposed to be virtuous . . . (i, p. 59)

This passage appears to suggest that sensibility is allied to, or even identical with, the innate love of truth which leads to the love of God and the development of virtue. Later the same day Mary is found reflecting that although sensibility 'produces flights of virtue', it needs to be 'curbed by reason' if it is not to develop into 'vice talking, and even thinking of virtue' (i, p. 61). Again, she confidently asserts that her 'involuntary' affections, 'fixed by reflection', produce beneficial effects and lead her from love of her fellow creatures to love of 'the Author of all Perfection' (i, p. 46); but it is clearly her sensibility which is responsible for her anguished feeling that she is 'particularly susceptible of misery' as well as of 'the most rapturous emotions' (i, p. 57).

The solution to the problem lies in the fact that in this tormented state she feels that her reason – that faculty which alone can modify violent feelings which will otherwise take control – has deserted her. Treated with irony, or at least discussed critically, this could be an extremely interesting issue: a 'thinking' woman, who prides herself on her rationality and self-control, finds that her emotions are more powerful than she had anticipated. But Wollstonecraft never overtly makes this point, and there is nothing to suggest that she followed her arguments through to this obvious conclusion. Her main problem, it could be said, apart from all the technical difficulties, is in the title: by calling the work *Mary* she both calls attention to and defines the problem. She cannot separate herself from the heroine or separate herself or the heroine from the narrator – all three are merely aspects, and not really even different aspects, of the same ego and mind. Each defines and reinforces the others, and there is no possibility of character revelation in action or in thought, since there is no distance between writer and subject, and no space in which characters can establish themselves or act in their own right. They act only to illustrate what the author/narrator is thinking and feeling.

Mary is a novel of wish-fulfilment, of sentimentalism, the portrait of a heroine as martyr who sacrifices herself in the interest of higher things. She seeks death, and finds death interesting: she has a fascination with melancholia, disappointment and suffering which is wholly at odds with the supposedly healthy strength of mind which Wollstonecraft apparently wanted to demonstrate. In spite of – or because of – her cultivation of sensibility, she wills a life beyond the physical, rejecting the life of the body in an attempt to strengthen the spiritual.

Wollstonecraft seems to lack invention, and the plot is flagged forward, the introspection losing touch with the narrative as if the narrative hangs on the passages of discursive meditation rather than the plot giving rise to them. It is heavily didactic, yet leads only to negativity and death. Even a happy ending, which she refuses, would have suggested positive social action rather than the withdrawal into egotistical chimeras which she chooses. The lyricism and the recently acquired intellectual and literary references cannot sustain the action in the face of such a tenuous grasp of the actual surfaces of life. Mary functions neither as a rational woman contrasted with the irrationality of her mother nor as a woman of feeling and sensibility, since she is far too self-regarding to be either. Little is enacted or dramatised; most is told by the insistent, moralising narrator, who is generally aware of no one's virtue but her own. 'She had not any prejudices,' says Wollstonecraft of Mary, 'for every opinion was examined before it was adopted' (i, p. 29), but in practice this is far from the case. Within a few chapters we meet prejudices about foreigners, particularly Roman Catholic foreigners – as in Chapter 14, which describes the barbarism of the Portuguese, who cannot control their revenge or their lust, and have no respect for thought or intellect. Her reaction to them is, in fact, at one with what she condemns: she says they are gross, she is disgusted by them (i, p. 36).

She is also disgusted by the body of her husband, and turns from bodies and bodily worship to Henry, who is all mind and soul and who, since he is dying, will soon be all soul. Henry is as sentimental a portrait of a swain as ever appeared in the novels she condemns: he is manly and restrained, except for his occasional sighing, and the fact that he is ill and dying before her very eyes makes him irresistibly attractive. Despite her religion she is secular enough to conclude that life would not, after all, be a vale of tears if she had Henry on a permanent basis, but of course he dies in her arms, and she is left with the disgust of being with her husband. This is certainly resignation, but perhaps also self-immolation. It is hard to see this solution as moral, however conventional it may be. Critically, *Mary* sank like a stone, and it is hardly surprising.

By 13 September 1787, Wollstonecraft had decided to move to London and put her 'new plan of life' into action (Wardle (1979) p. 159). 'Mr Johnson . . . assures me that if I exert my talents in writing I may support myself in a comfortable way', she wrote to her sister Everina in November (Wardle (1979) p. 164). By 15 November she was settled at 49 George Street, 'a little house, in a street near Black-Friars Bridge', *Mary* had been given to Johnson, and she was working on 'another book for young people, which I think has some merit' (Wardle (1979) p. 166). This, presumably, was *Original Stories from Real Life; with Conversations Calculated to Regulate the Affections, and Form the Mind to Truth and Goodness*, which was published in April 1788.

Original Stories proved to be an extremely popular work: a second edition, with six illustrations designed and engraved by Blake, appeared in 1791, and the work was still being reissued in 1835. Clearly based partly on Wollstonecraft's own experiences as governess to the Kingsboroughs' daughters as well as at Newington Green, it also met a demand for books which would both entertain and educate children. A very large number of such works had appeared in the previous twenty years. One of the first was Sarah Fielding's *The Governess* (1749), which went through six editions by 1781, the declared aim of which was 'to cultivate an early inclination to Benevolence, and a love of Virtue, in the Minds of Young Women', in order that they might find happiness in 'any of the Stations of Life allotted to the Female Character' (p. [iii]).

The 1780s had seen a proliferation of similarly 'improving' books for children. Wollstonecraft's acquaintance Anna Barbauld had published *Hymns in Prose for Children* in 1781. Wollstonecraft had also met the successful children's author Sarah Trimmer, whom she described as 'a truly respectable woman' (Wardle (1979) p. 166), and whose *Fabulous Histories* (1786) – better known as *History of the Robins* – is described by the children in *Original Stories* as 'a pretty book' (although their governess warns them not to be beguiled into thinking that birds talk). Another popular series by 'Mrs Teachwell' (Eleanor Fenn) included *The Female Guardian* (1784) and *Moral and Instructive Tales for the Improvement of Young Ladies* (1786). Wollstonecraft also knew Thomas Day's hugely popular *Sandford and Merton* (vol. i 1783, vol. ii 1786), which she describes in the *Rights of Woman* as 'one of the most instructive books that our country has produced for children (v, p. 109). Although her *Analytical* review of the third volume of *Sandford and Merton* (1789) postdates *Original Stories* by eighteen months, her comments give a clear indication of the virtues she found in Day's work, which she had presumably hoped to emulate in her own. She praises his lack of dogmatism and his practical, amusing and instructive illustrations of 'the first principles of morality', which gradually unfold to the child the value of 'humanity, honour, true courage, and universal benevolence'. He avoids the faults which she finds in other popular children's authors, who advocate blind observance of filial and religious duties, which, she writes, 'must ever give the mind an indolent, servile turn'. Day's writings, on the other hand, make obvious to a child 'the real dignity of man' (vii, p. 175).

Clearly the writing of children's literature was largely, though not exclusively, dominated by women writers; in addition, many of the works were aimed at the education of girls.[4] A recent commentator has argued that Wollstonecraft's governess narrator, Mrs Mason, 'typifies a whole body of female authority figures' who appear in these works, and demonstrate a 'new mode of female heroism . . . rationality, self-command, moral authority' (Myers (1986) pp. 54, 34). While there is undeniably some truth in this statement, Wollstonecraft's emphasis in *Original Stories* is noticeably different from that of other writers. In this work she lays particular stress on the development of inner qualities, arguing that the 'mind and heart' are capable of improvement, a 'perfectibilist' view that is not found in any other contemporary work of this nature.

Wollstonecraft's Preface sets her work apart from that of other writers of similar works. It is exceptional both for being militant and for explaining the author's educational theories in some detail. Wollstonecraft seems deliberately to have set out to flout the convention of introducing books aimed at children with polite addresses to their parents: her letter to Johnson, refusing his request that she alter the Preface, makes this clear: 'I . . . have not altered it. I hate the usual smooth way of exhibiting proud humility' (Wardle (1979) p. 167). Johnson's fear that she would offend her readers is understandable. The Preface begins by describing 'the present state of society, which obliges the author to attempt to cure those faults by reason, which ought never to have taken root in the infant mind'. Good habits would have been preferable to the precepts of reason, but to instil these 'requires more judgment than generally falls to the lot of parents' (iv, p. 359).

She dissociates herself both from aristocratic writing and from the effusions of 'feminine' style: her aim, she says, is 'perspicuity and simplicity of style', and an attempt to avoid 'unmeaning compliments' and 'false politeness' which sacrifices 'sincerity . . . and truth' (*ibid.*). Even when she moves on to a discussion of educational theory, she is irresistibly led back to the failings of parents. Knowledge should ideally come from example rather than teaching, and be addressed to the senses:

> But to wish that parents would, themselves, mould the ductile passions, is a chimerical wish, for the present generation have their own passions to combat with, and fastidious pleasures to pursue, neglecting those pointed out by nature: we must therefore pour premature knowledge into the succeeding one; and, teaching virtue, explain the nature of vice. Cruel necessity! (*ibid.*)

As a whole, the Preface seems extremely – unnecessarily – abrasive and aggressive. Wollstonecraft runs the risk of antagonising potential buyers by insulting them, and seems to think that abuse is the opposite of the 'proud humility' which she rejects.

Wollstonecraft ends the Preface with a statement of the work's aims: 'to fix principles of truth and humanity on a solid and simple foundation', and to lead a child to a comprehension of the 'dignity and happiness' to be derived from 'imitating' God, 'the Supreme Being . . . , recognised as the Universal Father, the Author and Centre of Good' (iv, p. 360). Nothing so ambitious is to be found in the works of her contemporaries, who are generally content to express a hope of cultivating Christian benevolence and a love of virtue. Even when 'devotional feelings' are explicitly mentioned, no writer comes near to Wollstonecraft's boldness in suggesting that a child should be encouraged actually to model herself on God, as Wollstonecraft's Mrs Mason also does in the work itself.

Original Stories concerns the moral education of Mary, aged 14, and Caroline, aged 12, by their governess, Mrs Mason. The introduction explains that because the children have been neglected by their parents and brought up by servants, they are 'shamefully ignorant' and prejudiced. They are possessed of 'tolerable capacities', but Mary is too fond of ridicule and Caroline is vain (iv, p. 361). Mrs Mason's plan for their improvement is based on the understanding that she will be with them at all times, and allow them to ask as many questions as they like. Her method seems carefully planned to include approaches aimed at all the faculties which Wollstonecraft felt to be important in the educational process: reasoned arguments to convince the intellect; demonstrations and evidence, often drawn from the natural world, which is vividly described in Wollstonecraft's prose, to address the senses ('the first inlets to the heart' (iv, p. 359)); and illustrative stories to enliven the imagination. In this her emphasis appears to have shifted somewhat from her arguments in *The Education of Daughters*: in that work the stress was chiefly on reason, whereas *Original Stories* promotes learning by habit and example. Mrs Mason shows her approval or disapproval of the children's behaviour by bestowing or withholding her affection; but apart from this there is mercifully little in the way of learning by means of reward and punishment, a method which figures largely in the works of some of Wollstonecraft's contemporaries. In the stories themselves, however, reward and punishment appear in a broader sense, since the good come to good ends and the bad to bad ones.

The work contains twenty-five chapters, each of which is designed to encourage the development of a particular virtue or to discourage a particular vice. Again, the scope of Mrs Mason's concerns is ambitious and impressive. Even the more conventional virtues are recommended for their value in the girls' personal development: kindness to animals because it forms the basis of benevolence, and thus extends first to our fellow men and then to the love of God (Chapters i–iii), and good behaviour to servants because it develops 'True Dignity of Character' (Chapter xii). In addition, Wollstonecraft ventures into areas where no other writer has gone before. She suggests, for example, that 'Cultivation of the Fancy raises us above the Vulgar, extends our Happiness, and leads to Virtue' (Chapter xiii). It would be a mistake, however, to read too much into Wollstonecraft's recommendation of the imagination in *Original Stories*: at this stage in her life she seems to view it chiefly as leading to the acquisition of 'taste', a thoroughly eighteenth-century view which bears little relation to the way in which her ideas developed a few years later. But *Original Stories* does show that she had already begun to absorb the radical political ideas of the intellectuals whom she had met through Johnson: most of the poverty and suffering for which the girls' charity and compassion are invited is shown to be a result of the oppression of tyrannical landlords (iv, pp. 375, 419–20) or of social injustices, especially to members of the armed forces (iv, pp. 397, 433); and one story includes a description of the sufferings of the 'poor wretches' in the 'dreadful' jail in France where they are kept in 'comfortless solitude' (iv, p. 376).

Mrs Mason reinforces her lessons by introducing the girls to various female acquaintances – allegorical figures, in fact, as their names suggest – whom they may wish to emulate. Mrs Trueman is the ideal wife and mother. She is possessed of 'an accomplished and dignified mind, that relies on itself'; she takes pleasure in drawing, music, and a 'bookcase full of well-chosen books'; and her evenings are given over to a combination of self-improvement, wifely devotion and maternal duties:

> Her husband, a man of taste and learning, reads to her, while she makes clothes for her children, whom she teaches in the tenderest, and most persuasive manner, important truths and elegant accomplishments. (iv, p. 386)

Her life is deliberately contrasted with that of her cousin Lady Sly, whose unhappiness, despite her greater wealth, is shown to be a result of her own lack of mental and moral cultivation:

> [She] has a little soul, she never attended to truth, and obtaining a great part of her fortune by falsehood, it has blighted all her enjoyments. . . . Her suspicious temper arises from a lack of knowledge of her own heart . . . (iv, p. 385)

Elsewhere in the work, Mrs Mason makes a general statement about marriage which reinforces these views:

Respect for the understanding must be the basis of constancy; the tenderness which flows from pity is liable to perish insensibly, to consume itself – even the virtues of the heart, when they degenerate into weakness, sink a character in our estimation. Besides, a kind of gross familiarity takes the place of domestic affection; and the respect which alone can render domestic intimacy a lasting comfort is lost before we are aware of it. (iv, p. 411)

Companionship in an affectionate marriage is obviously Mrs Mason's ideal; but *Original Stories* is the first of Wollstonecraft's works to contain examples of women who have succeeded in making satisfactory lives for themselves despite their single status. Anna Lofty, the village schoolmistress, who has been left poor and friendless after the death of her father, rejects the offer of a wealthy but loveless marriage, and determines to make her way alone:

She had her father's spirit of independence, and determined to shake of[f] the galling yoke which she had long struggled with, and try to earn her own subsistence. Her acquaintance expostulated with her, and represented the miseries of poverty, and the mortifications and difficulties that she would have to encounter. Let it be so, she replied, it is much preferable to swelling the train of the proud or vicious great. . . . My wants are few. When I am my own mistress, the crust I earn will be sweet, and the water that moistens it will not be mingled with tears of sorrow or indignation. (iv, p. 428)

Finally, of course, there is Mrs Mason herself, strong, rational and self-controlled. If Anna Lofty represents one facet of Wollstonecraft's self-image, Mrs Mason surely represents another, although it is difficult to see her as being as stern and unbending as her fictional governess. But the girls themselves, although they are very much in awe of Mrs Mason, also seem to be devoted to her.[5] In any case, Mrs Mason does have a more human side, which reveals itself as the work progresses: in Chapter xv, for instance, she allows the girls a glimpse of her own past circumstances:

early attachments have been broken – the death of friends I loved has . . . clouded my days. . . . [My heart] has often been wounded by ingratitude; my fellow creatures, whom I have fondly loved, have neglected me . . . (iv, p. 422)

Despite – or more probably because of – these early disappointments,

Mrs Mason is strong on fortitude and endurance. In Chapter xxi, entitled 'The Benefit of Bodily Pain – Fortitude the Basis of Virtue – the Folly of Irresolution', she argues that:

> it is the patient endurance of pain that will enable you to resist your passions; after you have borne bodily pain, you will have firmness enough to sustain the still more excruciating agonies of the mind. (iv, p. 438)

She makes an interesting linguistic point: 'The term virtue, comes from a word signifying strength': 'Fortitude of mind is, therefore, the basis of every virtue, and virtue belongs to a being that is weak in its nature, and strong only in will and resolution' (iv, p. 437). This is the essence of Wollstonecraft's teaching, at least in her early works: she anticipates Jane Austen in placing the highest possible value on the development of 'self-command' and inner strength. Mrs Mason, indeed, believes that goodness consists in endeavouring to copy the attributes of the Creator (iv, p. 423). We may not warm to her – she has no sense of fun, and little or no understanding of what it is like to be a child – but it is impossible not to admire her extraordinary strengths. Her authority and her independence, combined with her development of 'female' virtues of nurture and sensitivity, represent an important step forward in the presentation of women in literature. But that Wollstonecraft was, at this stage, still firmly rooted in the eighteenth century is obvious in the violent contrast between her view of children and their needs, and that of Blake, who illustrated *Original Stories* in 1791.

Blake's children live in light, but are dragged by adults into darkness: for him, children are naturally good and naturally happy, but adults force a world of evil and misery on them. As a Romantic, he cannot help subverting Wollstonecraft's text. His Mrs Mason shares the world of the children. She is young and slender and ethereal, like them, and completely unlike Wollstonecraft's didactic, cheerless original, who can crush a lark with her foot (iv, p. 369) and who inculcates in the children the fear of God rather than the love of Christ. A story about a meeting with a Welsh Harper, told by Wollstonecraft's Mrs Mason as an illustration of the tyranny of landlords and the virtues of charity, becomes entirely different in Blake's illustration: his Welsh Harper (iv, p. 417) is an angelic vision of light surrounded by a world of darkness and rocky inhospitality, gazed at by an enamoured Mrs Mason (demure but subdued sexually) who is struck silent with admiration, overcome with passion. In Chapter xxiv, Mrs Mason takes the girls to visit a poor family in London, to demonstrate once again the value of charity. Blake is obviously (and for obvious reasons) unimpressed by Mrs Mason's insistence that 'Oeconomy and self-denial are necessary in every station, to enable us to be generous' (iv, p. 445), and his illustrative plate shows the whole family descending into the depths of misery and despair in a dreadful garret (iv, p. 447). Blake is always on the side of children, of love, of joy and of Innocence; Mrs Mason seems in many respects to belong to the world of Experience. It has been argued that Wollstonecraft represents the ideal woman of Blakean Romanticism (Gaunt (1956) pp. 77–8, 86–90). But while Wollstone-craft's life may have had some bearing on the Mary of Blake's poem 'Mary', his views of Innocence and Experience are radically different from anything that she has to say about children and their education at this stage.

In dramatising Mrs Mason, Wollstonecraft is obviously drawing to some extent on herself and her own experiences, but she also has an eye on the public, and the need to construct a figure who will embody discipline as well as understanding. She is learning to tell stories, to construct narrative which will sustain a consistent viewpoint, to inculcate morals while questioning accepted standards, and to find a public who will buy her work. Her problem is the problem of all who try to live by writing: to be themselves, and honest with themselves, while selling themselves to a largely conservative public. She tries out various methodologies in these tales and gets away, to some extent, from the epistolary style that chokes the narrative of *Mary*. She begins to develop particular themes, such as the tyranny of landowners towards their tenants, although her own stance – as embodied in Mrs Mason's – remains aloof and aristocratic, that of a moral Lady Bountiful.

How far and how fast Wollstonecraft's ideas progressed in a relatively short time may be gauged through comparing these early works on education with her *Lessons* ('which I intended to have written for my unfortunate girl'), which were published by Godwin in Volume II of Wollstonecraft's *Posthumous Works*. Godwin's note suggests that they were written in October 1795, but they must surely have been completed at a later date, as Fanny was then only 18 months old, and Lesson V refers to her as being 4 (iv, p. 469). *Lessons* also

include references to baby William, the name Godwin and Wollstonecraft used for their unborn child, which suggests that she was working
on the book during the last months of her life. It has been suggested
that these *Lessons* were merely reading lessons (Wardle (1951) p. 301),
which seems unlikely in view of the material. The first three chapters
are lists of words; the rest are short sentences which are too difficult
for a child of 3 or 4 to master, although she might understand them
if they were read to her, especially since they explore a child's world
in, for the most part, a child's language.

The *Lessons* have all that Wollstonecraft's earlier educational works
lack. They exemplify love – above all empathy, compassion, and care
in a very practical sense: care that belongs with love, in case the child
should swallow pins or play with knives, for instance; and care that
teaches to care for others, such as not making a noise when someone
is asleep or unwell. They also have a sense of the connections that
love builds between mother, father and child, and that age builds
between baby, child, children and adults; and those that build
between generations. The stages of growth – from suckling, to
teething and weaning, to the development of consciousness – are
simply, directly and practically presented:

> You know much more than William, now you walk alone, and talk;
> but you do not know as much as the boys and girls you see playing
> yonder, who are half as tall again as you; and they do not know half as
> much as their mothers and fathers, who are men and women grown.
> Papa and I were children, like you; and men and women took care of
> us. (iv, p. 472)

The language enters the consciousness of the child. 'Good' and 'bad'
are not moral concepts at all, they are simply knowledge: the child
learns that hard fruit makes her sick, for instance; and as she grows
older, so she grows wiser, practically speaking. She learns to help
those, like the puppy, who cannot help themselves, while also
learning that she needs help to do those things she cannot yet manage.
But she is part of a circle of growth, generation and love which
embraces all things in a world that is almost entirely domestic. As she
moves in Lessons I, II and III from nouns (things) to verbs (actions),
to abstractions, sentences and thinking, so the child's progress is
plotted towards self-sufficiency, understanding and compassion,
without didacticism, morality or right and wrong (except in a purely
practical sense) arising at all.

As a mother Wollstonecraft has learnt what as a teacher, governess and theorist she never learnt: that the great secret of morals – to quote her future son-in-law, Shelley – is love. She does not feel the need to preach or rationalise, only to love and protect her child. The language, like the message, could not be simpler, more direct, more normal and less artificial: a mother addressing her child is the most complete form of communication, emotionally, intellectually, and physically – mother and child confront each other without guile, with frankness, honesty and love and, most importantly, with complete but implicit trust. Previously in Wollstonecraft's works, the teacher has distrusted the children. Now the mother trusts her child, watches her learn to care for herself and for others, but trusts too that she will grow morally without didacticism, without a system of rewards and punishments. She learns from her own experience: 'You asked me for some apples when your stomach ached; I was not angry with you. If you had been as wise as Papa . . .' (iv, p. 474). Wollstonecraft's attitude towards children has been changed – virtually reversed. So has her style, which is now strong, simple, direct and confident. Good, wishful warmth surrounds the ideal family group: Mamma, Papa, baby William and Fanny – Wollstonecraft was incurably domestic to the end, despite her radicalism. But the central fact about *Lessons* is that the consciousness of the child is re-enacted verbally: from objects, to actions, to abstractions and discriminations. Wollstonecraft has come to rest in Romantic assumptions regarding children and childhood, and she has found the authentic voice of feeling.

Chapter 2

◆

The Analytical Review (1788–92)

By the time Wollstonecraft moved to London at the end of 1787, Johnson had already begun to plan the new literary periodical which he, as publisher, and Thomas Christie, as editor, established in May 1788 as *The Analytical Review*. Indeed, part of Johnson's reason for inviting her to London and providing a home for her was presumably the fact that she could be useful to him as a reviewer. Her friendship with Johnson developed quickly, and he describes it in the note he wrote for Godwin when he was preparing *Memoirs*:

> During her stay at George St she spent many of her afternoons, and some of her evenings with me. She was incapable of disguise, whatever was the state of her mind it appeared when she entered and the turn of conversation might be easily guessed; when harassed which was very often the case, she was relieved by unbosoming herself and generally returned home calm, frequently in spirits. F[useli] was frequently with us.[1]

Clearly she relied on Johnson as patron, friend and confidant; indeed, she wrote to him at the time that he was 'the only person I am intimate with – I never had a father or a brother – you have been both to me' (Wardle (1979) p. 178). She learnt much of her radicalism from him, Fuseli and their circle: of the books published on the French Revolution between July 1789 and December 1791, thirteen at least were published by Johnson, including those by Wollstonecraft herself, Thomas Christie and Joseph Priestley; also Thomas Paine's

Rights of Man, although it was published by J. Jordan, was originated by Johnson.

She must have met Christie at this time,[2] although nothing is known of their early relationship. They were about the same age (Christie was born in 1761), although he was better known and much better established, being well connected – a friend of Anna Seward, Joseph Priestley and John Nichols, among others. He was well read in English and continental literature, which 'suggested to [him] the first outline of a Review of Books upon the *Analytical* plan' (Nichols (1812–15) ix, p. 388). He was enthusiastic about the French Revolution; he went to Paris at the end of 1789 and spent six months there, and on his return he published *A Sketch of the New Constitution of France* (1790) and *Letters on the Revolution of France, and the New Constitution Established by the National Assembly* (1791), which Wollstonecraft quoted extensively and verbatim in her *Historical and Moral View of . . . the French Revolution* a few years later. He returned to Paris in 1792, and was employed by the Assembly on the English translation of the proposed polyglot edition of the Revolutionary Constitution: in the event, only his translation and the Italian were ever published (3 vols, Paris, 1792). He had married Rebecca Thomson in September 1792, and his wife went to Paris with him. Wollstonecraft met them there, though when is not clear. After her suicide attempt in 1795 she seems to have recovered at his house.

The *Analytical* was not the first periodical to be devoted solely to reviews: both *The Monthly Review,* founded in 1749, and *The Critical Review,* founded in 1756, had by the 1780s been given over entirely to the reviewing of newly published books. Christie's pre-publication Advertisement announced that the *Analytical* would differ from the other journals: it would give its readers a chance to judge books for themselves by providing full analytical accounts, unencumbered by too many critical remarks, of all works of importance. Although, he argued, this had been the practice of the other journals in their early days, more recent critics 'have filled their publications with little else than their opinions and judgements' (*Analytical Review* 1, p. [i]). The Advertisement carried a statement of the policy which it expected of its reviewers:

> In the judgements given on books, the writers will endeavour to conduct themselves with that degree of modesty which is most suitable to their character. Where absurdity and immorality are attempted to

> be imposed on the public, they will certainly think themselves authorized to raise the rod of criticism, but will not deem themselves entitled to interfere in a dictatorial manner, when authors of approved learning and genius have produced a work containing an elaborate chain of facts and arguments, nor pretend by the hasty reading of an hour to confute the labour of years. (*Analytical Review* 1, pp. iv–v)

In fact the *Analytical* never approached Christie's ideal of impartiality. Had it done so, this would certainly have made 'Anon.' reviewing more appropriate than signed reviews. This method was chosen presumably because it would also eliminate the suspicion – often voiced and often true – that reviewers were puffing books by their publisher or their friends. It would also eliminate the bias which was often felt to be part of reviewers' stock in trade. They would be impartial, and greater attention would be paid to the quality of the book reviewed than to the reviewer. The *Analytical* would indeed, according to Christie's Preface, ignore – or at least give titles only, or a 'very brief character' to – 'trifling and temporary' publications, while providing a 'large account . . . that in some degree conveyed to the reader the knowledge of the book' of the 'truly STANDARD works, which add to the stock of human knowledge, and will live beyond a day'. He also proposed some Literary News and some accounts of foreign literature, and in view of the fact that Wollstonecraft was brushing up her French and learning German, it is probable that she did some of these: reports, for example, of the proceedings of foreign societies and articles published in foreign journals (the amount of reading she must have done in order to produce her pieces is daunting). The *Analytical* was also – though Christie's Advertisement did not say so – more radical in its political views than either of the older publications. By the time of its demise in June 1799 it had done much to encourage the growth of Romanticism by giving sympathetic encouragement to the early poetry of Wordsworth, and publishing work by Lamb and Southey.

Wollstonecraft, already working for Johnson as a translator and writer, was apparently employed to write reviews as soon as the *Analytical* began publication, as her undated but presumably early letters to Johnson indicate (Wardle (1979) pp. 178, 179). Later she acted as assistant editor, commissioning reviews, and probably took over in 1790 during the six months or so that Christie spent in Paris.

The policy of the *Analytical*, in common with that of other periodical publications at this time, was to publish all its reviews anonymously. This had not, apparently, been Christie's original plan: a letter to him from Anna Seward expresses her approval of the reviewing being: 'a day-light business! To have the names of its authors and compilers known, will be great guards of its integrity' (quoted in Tyson (1979) p. 98). The change of policy was presumably due to the fact that reviewers demanded anonymity to protect them against defamation and libel. They felt that they could not be honest in their opinions unless they were protected in this way: thus 'Anon.' was a guarantee of integrity – not signatures, as Anna Seward suggests. The *Analytical* compromised largely by using letters, though these were clearly coded: presumably those in the know were aware of their meaning, but they stopped a long way short of signatures. The contributors wanted their identities hidden for another reason also: many of them were prominent and respected writers in their own right, and did not want to be identified with hack work turned out for the money alone. For the most part, they needed the work, and the money it brought them, but they did not want to be seen as part of Pope's Grub Street, particularly as such a reputation would rub off on their own writing.

Wollstonecraft probably contributed to the first two issues of the *Analytical*, in May and June 1788, but her first signed reviews (signed M and W, that is) appeared in the July issue.[3] They include a long review of Charlotte Smith's *Emmeline*, a four-volume novel, the effects of which she thought would certainly 'debauch the mind' of 'young females', thus demonstrating a greater concern for morality than for aesthetics or imagination.

Most of her reviews are in fact summaries of the books' contents with extracts and some judicial – though not always judicious – comment. The editors of her *Collected Works* say that she contributed about thirty-plus an issue (vii, p. 14), and are surely right when they say that they 'were probably written hurriedly' (vii, p. 17). They cover a surprising range of topics, though she responded most readily to educational books, books of a general nature on history, religion and morals, and novels. She also seems to have made a special effort to review travel books, as if in order to study the genre itself. She clearly earned a good deal of her income from these contributions.

In her early reviews she seldom speaks out in her own voice, but it is obvious from her later reviews, written after the success of *Rights of Woman*, that she grew in confidence and conviction as she became established. There is a movement from the orthodoxy of her early reviews to the challenging comments she sometimes introduces into her late ones – as when, for example, she deplores the style and affectations of Robert Mary's poem 'Laurel of Liberty', while at the same time praising his enthusiasm and the sentiments arising from his response to the French Revolution (vii, pp. 330–1). In her review of a new collection of letters by Rousseau, she warns biographers not to study their authors too minutely:

> It is not necessary to inquire how, or when, a great man combed his head, washed his face, or performed the common duties which cleanliness requires. We all know that he is a man, and it is an insult to our nature when these insignificant details are brought forward to notice. It is, indeed, a cruel affront to departed genius, to rake up every casual saying, and inconsiderate letter, under the invidious pretence of giving a faithful picture of a noble mind, when the real motive is to gratify the grovellers, who can only rise by deprecating others. (vii, pp. 362–3).

Her long review of John Hampson's *Memoirs of the late Rev. John Wesley* establishes her sympathy with earnestness, dedication and moral seriousness of a puritanical kind, Wesley being so much the reformer of morals and religion among 'the lower classes of people'. She welcomes the prospect of an advance 'through industry and sobriety, in their condition; and a considerable progress in knowledge and learning' (vii, p. 375).

Literary criticism

Although the range of subject matter which Wollstonecraft undertook to review for the *Analytical* quickly widened and diversified, novels nearly always seem to have been passed to her. In addition, she wrote a number of reviews of poetry, and some of published plays. As might be expected, her opinions were consistent, decided and strongly expressed: more so, it might be felt, than Christie's announcement allowed for. Her strongest views, however, were expressed chiefly on moral issues, for which Christie made an exception.

In the case of novels, her criticisms are based on two main grounds: probability and morality. In fact, these two are closely related: if a novel abounds in clichés and 'preposterous sentiments' (vii, p. 26) it will lead its readers to entertain false expectations about the nature of life and of love which will:

tend to debauch the mind, and throw an insipid kind of uniformity over the moderate and rational prospects of life, consequently *adventures* are sought for and created, when duties are neglected and content despised. (vii, p. 27)

Very few novels attain Wollstonecraft's high standard of excellence. Her reviews are peppered with lively epithets: '[a] tangled skein of nonsense' (vii, p. 135); 'this wretched farrago' (vii, p. 154); 'trash . . . whipped syllabub' (vii, p. 192); 'cold rant, and unintelligible nonsense' (vii, p. 284); 'one of the most stupid novels we have ever impatiently read. Pray, Miss, write no more!' (vii, p. 185). She disapproves rather less of tedious insipidity, foolishness and lack of imagination, which can at least be said to be 'harmless', than she does of affectation, artificiality, unnatural characters and overdone catastrophes, which may 'injure young minds by exhibiting life through a false medium' (vii, p. 66); but it is less easy to find examples of any qualities of which she wholeheartedly approves.

'Reality', or 'truth', seems to be one of her criteria for excellence. In a review (January 1789) lamenting the lack in most writers of the 'uncommon abilities' required to write a really good novel, she suggests that a writer of genius, such as Shakespeare, can invest his characters with such 'reality' that we accept even his monsters, 'thinking them new, though not unnatural'. This is presumably because his characters, like those of Richardson (whom she goes on to discuss), are:

made up of mortal passions, and are affected by those delicate shades and tints which suddenly give a glimpse of the heart, and tie the whole family on earth together. (vii, p. 66)

To make characters 'real', while it is highly desirable, is not enough. This seems clear from a review of Helen Maria Williams's *Julia* (1790). Wollstonecraft applauds Williams's simplicity, naturalness and ease, and finds her characters 'delineated with a degree of truth and proportion, which instantly insinuates that they were drawn from nature'; but she comments that the story is neither dramatic enough to excite the reader's sympathy nor complex enough to rouse their interest. While she cannot find fault with Williams's moral, she is disappointed with the work: the heroine is too high-principled for her safety ever to be in question. This leads Wollstonecraft to a conclusion which tends to contradict views which she has expressed elsewhere:

A good tragedy or novel, if the criterion be the effect which it has on the reader, is not always the most moral work, for it is not the reveries of sentiment, but the struggles of passion – of those *human passions*, that too frequently cloud the reason, and lead *mortals* into dangerous errors, if not into absolute guilt, which raise the most lively emotions, and leave the most lasting impression on the memory; an impression rather made by the heart than the understanding; for our affections are not quite so voluntary as the suffrage of reason. (vii, pp. 251–3)

In her review of Elizabeth Inchbald's *A Simple Story* (1791) she can find no fault with the dramatic qualities, the discriminating and observant characterisation, or the lively and spirited dialogue. But she laments the fact that the excellent moral ('to show the advantage of a good education') is not sufficiently reinforced by a more strongly drawn contrast between the two leading female characters, the mother and the daughter; and she attempts to correct Inchbald, wishing that the daughter had been given more 'dignity of mind'. It would have been better, she says, if she had been shown rising above her misfortunes and acquiring through her adversity a greater dignity of mind, rather than suffering her health to be undermined by 'the trials of her patience, which ought to have strengthened her understanding' (vii, p. 370). She sees the novel as primarily a didactic form, and though she praises Inchbald's style, 'the feminine ease that characterises the conversation of an agreeable well-bred woman', she – properly, perhaps – attacks her for poisoning the minds of their own sex, by strengthening 'a male prejudice that makes women system-atically weak':

Why do all female writers, even when they display their abilities, always give a sanction to the libertine reveries of men? . . . [by] the absurd fashion of making the heroine of a novel boast of a delicate constitution; and the still more ridiculous and deleterious custom of spinning the more picturesque scenes out of fevers, swoons, and tears. (vii, pp. 369–70)

This is only one of a number of occasions on which Wollstonecraft shows her irritation with female authors, who 'like timid sheep . . . jump over the hedge one after another, and would not dream of deviating either to the right or left' (vii p. 92), so that 'truth compels us to declare that we open a novel with a degree of pleasure when *written by a lady* is not inserted in the title page' (vii, p. 121).

One novel not 'written by a lady' to which Wollstonecraft accords reserved praise is Thomas Holcroft's *Anna St Ives* (1792). She is untroubled by the male authorship of a novel in which the central character is a woman. Although she detects in it a tendency to 'highly wrought pictures' which could, in the minds of the young and impressionable, spread 'a spice of romance', she feels that this will be outweighed by the fact that it so strongly recommends 'truth and many just opinions'. By this time, Wollstonecraft evidently shares what she calls Holcroft's 'democratical sentiments'; thus she can only speak in favour of the moral of his novel which, she believes, is calculated:

> to strengthen despairing virtue, to give fresh energy to the cause of humanity, to repress the pride and insolence of birth, and to shew that true nobility which can alone proceed from the head and the heart, claims genius and virtue for its armorial bearings, and, possessed of these, despises all the foppery of either ancient or modern heraldry. (vii, pp. 440–1)

Where poetry is concerned, Wollstonecraft's views are again firm and decided, and many of the ideas which she would express more fully in her essay 'On Poetry, and Our Relish for the Beauties of Nature' (1797) can be seen taking shape in her reviews. Truth, sincerity, and lack of affectation are important components, as they were in the case of the novel; but moral issues, which played such a large part in her criticism of fiction, have little direct bearing on her views on poetry. Indeed, she is strongly opposed to didactic poems, which she considers 'defective':

> because they want a prevailing interest to lead the reader on, and the whole hangs like a dead weight on the attention, sedulously employed to connect the scattered parts. (vii, p. 114)

She finds purely descriptive poetry 'tedious', because by definition it lacks a 'governing passion' to unite the various sentiments expressed (vii, pp. 112–13):

> We must follow the footsteps of a fellow creature, a social passion must connect the whole, to give warmth and continuity to our most refined instincts, or we flag, more particularly in cultivated scenes, more wild ones remind us of the *present God*; the soul asserts its dignity and claims kindred with the Being who inhabits the gloomy waste. (vii, p. 44)

This extract suggests that Wollstonecraft's criticism of poetry rests to some extent on criteria which were current throughout the eighteenth century: those of beauty and sublimity. It is clear, however, that for her – as for the Romantics a few years later – sublimity (the wild, the vast) has more appeal than the more civilised and orderly 'beautiful', which is in danger of appearing merely 'pretty' and 'elegant' – terms of mild disapprobation in her criticism. The quality she looks for in a work is 'a poetical enthusiastic glow which the reader would insensibly catch' (vii, p. 81). The 'pervading essence, bold imagery and elevated thoughts' which a poem contains make considerations of metre and correctness subordinate (vii, p. 94); indeed, it is possible to overlook faults or liberties taken with the diction if the poem is sufficiently energetic or beautiful (vii, p. 223).

None of the poetry which Wollstonecraft reviews for the *Analytical* comes up to her high standards of excellence. For the newly popular writers of the day she has only faint praise. William Lisle Bowles, a poet who was much admired by the young Coleridge, she finds simple and unaffected, but on the whole inferior to Charlotte Smith (vii, p. 87); she notes the 'melancholy cadence, which seems to be the natural tone of the author's mind' (vii, p. 224), but despite his 'elegiac sweetness' (vii, p. 421) she is evidently unimpressed by 'the only strain in which the writer pours out his mind' (vii, p. 422). Of Ann Yearsley, the briefly popular 'milkmaid of Bristol', she writes that she 'certainly has abilities', but her 'independent mind and feeling heart' are obscured by 'stale allusions', 'trite illustrations from classical lore' and a: 'confusion of thought, which shews struggling energy not strong enough to cultivate itself, and give form to a chaotic mass' (vii, p. 356).

For Wollstonecraft, Yearsley's poetry illustrates the fact that although, in a poet of true genius, the energy and imagination displayed will more than compensate for a disregard for rules and method, a weaker writer needs to be more scrupulous. Above all, however, she is troubled by Yearsley's 'vain kind of presumption' in claiming superiority as a poet purely on the basis of the praise with which her early works were greeted (vii, p. 398). Samuel Rogers's *Pleasures of Memory* (1792), a poem which became extremely popular (four editions appeared in the first year, and over 23,000 copies had been sold by 1816), is dismissed by Wollstonecraft in a few sentences: it is a 'little elegant poem', 'mellow' and 'tasteful', but 'neither the fiery stream of passion, nor the electric sparks of fancy burn along the lines' (vii, p. 432).

The strong emphasis which Wollstonecraft places on passion, or 'the passions', in her criticism of poetry may seem to contradict the resolute privileging of reason and self-control which has been met with elsewhere in her works. Perhaps the contradiction can be resolved by referring to the *Rights of Woman*, where she ventures to contradict 'men who have coolly seen mankind through the medium of books', and to assert that it is not always wise to regulate the passions. She suggests that if men sometimes appear to have 'superior judgement and more fortitude than women', it is owing to the fact that they give:

> freer scope to the grand passions, and by more frequently going astray enlarge their minds. If then by the exercise of their own reason they fix on some stable principle, they probably have to thank the force of their passions, nourished by *false* views of life, and permitted to overleap the boundary that secures content. (v, p. 179)

In other words, learning is best achieved through experience, even if that experience is painful. In addition, she argues that all the secondary passions entertained by 'short-sighted mortals' are merely weak reflections of, or preparations for, 'the governing passion implanted in us by the Author of all good', which is to perfect oneself in the knowledge and love of God (v, pp. 180–1). Finally, wisdom and compassion can be attained only by someone who has struggled with his own passions, so that he can judge 'the force of the temptation which betrayed his brother into vice' (v, p. 181). Presumably she may have believed that poetry, by enlivening the imagination, can reproduce the experience of the passions, and so produce the same valuable effects.

The critical principles which Wollstonecraft applies in her poetry reviews, although they are not strikingly original, appear to anticipate in many respects the criticism of the Romantic period. She places a high value on imagination and feeling, and correspondingly less on elegance, delicacy and correctness. The poets she admires most are Shakespeare, to whose 'magic powers' (vii, p. 224) and 'daring flights' (vii, p. 306) she returns again and again as a standard of true genius; and Milton, 'that sublime poet' whose design, 'calling forth a sublime glow of admiration, makes us feel he is true to nature' (vii, p. 348). Her stringent requirement that novels should have a sound moral gets little emphasis in her poetry reviews, although she is extremely critical of Pope's *Eloisa to Abelard*, on the grounds that:

Instead of passionate sorrow and tender melancholy, delicately though forcibly expressed, he paints cold licentiousness in the most elegant drapery, and bursts of anguish, to show his powers, are turned into romantic descriptions which fall in dying cadences on the ear. (vii, p. 436)

It is clear that she expects poetry to elevate the sensitive reader on to a higher plane where, being in tune with the beauty and sublimity of nature, they will naturally entertain what she sees as healthy, positive sentiments.

Travel literature

Wollstonecraft's critical comments on the increasingly popular genre of travel literature are of interest, if only because she went on to write her own travel book. Her reviews make it clear that she has no time for writers who are content simply to give 'heightened description[s] of . . . trifle[s]' (vii, p. 107); a work meets her approval if it indicates that the writer has 'travelled to extend the sphere of his thoughts, and, by sagacious comparisons, to fix sound results in his mind' (*ibid.*). She is unimpressed by Hester Lynch Piozzi's *Observations and Reflections, made in the Course of a Journey through France, Italy and Germany* (1789). Although she finds Piozzi's descriptions lively and amusing, she is dissatisfied with what she sees as her frivolity and superficiality, and judges the work as 'very desultory', having:

all the lax freedom of letters without that kind of insinuating interest, which slightly binds a nosegay of unconnected remarks, and throws a thin, but graceful veil over egotism. . . . (vii, p. 109)

She approves rather more of William Gilpin, whose writings on picturesque beauty were so highly influential at the time. In her review of his *Observations on the River Wye* (1789) she expresses her gratitude for the fact that Gilpin has 'some decided point in view, a grand object' to connect his reflections, instead of 'rambling with an unfixed eye through a variety of desultory matter and detached observations' (vii, p. 161). She has doubts, however, about his principles of picturesque beauty. She wonders if it is possible to reduce to principles, and transmit, something so 'evanescent and almost incommunicable', since it depends so much on the mood of the beholder (*ibid*.). In addition, she finds his illustrative drawings lacking in 'nerve and boldness in the lines', and is unhappy about the colours, which sometimes 'appear artificial and unnatural, though we are convinced they are not so': the problem arises from the lack of space available, which also, she feels, makes his sketches appear beautiful more often than sublime (vii, p. 162). A review of one of Gilpin's other works takes up the same subject. Tinted drawings, she argues, appear more artificial and diminutive than 'plain, shadowy drawings'; but many people are deceived by prettiness and 'childish neatness' which, however, simply amuses the senses while 'the imagination remains quiet' (vii, p. 197).

The only travel books to which Wollstonecraft gives her unqualified approval are those which are interspersed with 'historical facts and philosophical reflections', and so blend instruction and amusement by giving 'the natural history of the place and its inhabitants' (vii, p. 180). She likes William Hamilton's *Letters Concerning the Northern Coast of the County of Antrim* (1790), which she finds amusing, informative, intelligent and thought-provoking. She is particularly impressed with his 'volcanic theory of the basalts': that is, the idea that the Giant's Causeway was formed of volcanic lava which, over a long period of time, subsided into bold but regular formations. Hamilton's theory depends, however, on the supposition that the world was created at 'a period infinitely remote from the present age', and, '*many*, very many ages, before man . . . surveyed the wonders that had long unseen been changing':

> But if the earth was created for the habitation of intelligent beings –
> 'and that it was, all nature cries aloud', – why was so much time to be
> lost before the God of nature received the homage of a creature who
> could pant to resemble him? (vii, p. 278)

Despite the troublesome insolubility of such questions, she is grateful for a work which gives her so much subject for thought, and differs so greatly from the kind of affected, sentimental travel books which 'leave the understanding to starve' (vii, p. 279). Her irritation with the proliferation of such inferior works is clear in a review (October 1790) in which she notes that one of Bacon's essays had expressed the wish that all travellers would keep a journal:

> Were he now alive, he would have no reason to complain, for every
> inch of the continent has been described with scrupulous exactness,

and flying and loitering, sprightly and *vapourish* travellers, have given us, in their minute diaries . . . different views of the objects, which enables them to *while-a-way* some leisure time which hung heavy on their hands . . . (vii, p. 301)

Education and morality

Wollstonecraft's experience as a writer of books on education must have made her seem an obvious choice as a reviewer both of books aimed at children – like her *Original Stories* – and of books which discussed the theory of education, as she had done in the *Education of Daughters*.

Not surprisingly, Wollstonecraft has strong opinions about the kinds of books she considers suitable for children. She is in favour of works which provide useful lessons by example; always pragmatic in her views, she sees little point in preaching theories to children who are too young to understand them:

> *Children* are not to be excited to virtue, by hearing that life is but a dream, and that the human heart is naturally depraved. – Can they understand this language, or annex any ideas to the words? (vii, p. 35)

Worldly maxims may, indeed, be actively harmful to young children, since they have 'a greater tendency to narrow than enlarge the understanding, to teach suspicion rather than inspire benevolence'; she is particularly troubled by the practice of attempting to inculcate morality and virtue by means of 'slavish fear' of the Devil (vii, p. 292).

She disapproves of the practice of addressing children as grown persons, which tends to make them into '*forced* plants, hastily polished and hurried into manhood, to gratify the vanity of weak parents and the interested views of schoolteachers' (vii, p. 292), arguing that they should be addressed in language which is suited to their stage of development. As in the case of novels, she is strongly opposed to children's books containing affected language and sentiments which 'appear to have no heart in them', and may lead children to catch a 'prim hypocritical manner, the very reverse of that playful innocent sincerity, which is the chief charm of youth' (vii, p. 123–4).

The important issue of women's education, which forms the basis of much of the discussion in the *Rights of Woman*, is raised several times in her reviews, and it seems probable that her ideas on the subject were sharpened and clarified as a result. In June 1789 she quotes with approval from a writer who:

> exclaims against the present mode of polishing and indulging women, till they become weak and helpless beings, equally unnerved in body and mind: and hence infers, that gentleness, or rather the affectation of sickly feminine sensibility, indiscriminately wears away not only the strength but identity of character . . . (vii, p. 109)

In her 1790 review of *Sandford and Merton* (discussed in Chapter 1) she quotes a long extract on the subject, on which she expresses herself to be 'perfectly coinciding with [Day] in opinion', since:

> he wishes to see women educated as rational creatures, and not made mere polished playthings, to amuse the leisure hours of men. Trying to acquire feminine graces, and the sensibility so warmly recommended, women, indeed, may be termed with propriety, overgrown children; nay, to such an excess is this folly carried, that they glory in their weakness, giving it the softened name of delicacy; in short, many publications addressed to the *fair sex*, tend to make them artificial, useless characters. (vii, pp. 175–6)

Wollstonecraft's longest review on the subject of education is the one she wrote in November 1790 on Catherine Macaulay's *Letters on Education. With Observations on Religious and Metaphysical Subjects.* The review makes it clear that Macaulay's considerable achievements (a 'masculine and fervid writer' (vii, p. 309)) were as important to Wollstonecraft as the actual content of her work, since they display: 'a degree of sound reason and profound thought which either through defective organs, or mistaken education, seldom appears in female productions' (vii, p. 322).[4]

Wollstonecraft finds herself in perfect agreement with Macaulay not only in respect of the importance of the subject of education but also in her assertion that 'morals must be taught on immutable principles' (*ibid.*). She disagrees with her, however, on a number of minor points, and clearly finds her work deficient at times, mainly because of her lack of emphasis on certain issues, particularly that of parity of education for both sexes. Wollstonecraft agrees, for example, that a private education by enlightened parents is preferable to a public one, which may produce a brilliant mind and provide useful connections but will not 'fix just principles' in the mind (vii, p. 310); but she believes Macaulay is wrong in asserting that it is easy to find reliable and trustworthy tutors and governesses in whom parents can place full confidence. She wholeheartedly agrees with her emphasis on the importance of 'acquiring hardy habits', and with her belief that 'the amusements and instruction of boys and girls should be the same' (vii, p. 311). Indeed, she feels that Macaulay could have enlarged considerably on the subject treated in one of her chapters, 'No characteristic difference in sex', and considers that her reflections on female chastity, albeit accurate, require further explanation: 'for till the minds of women are more enlarged, we should not weaken the salutary prejudices which serve as a substitute, a weak one we own, for salutary principles' (vii, p. 314).

It should be clear from the discussions of Wollstonecraft's earlier writings that her educational theories were firmly rooted in her view of the purpose of human existence. The very pursuit of intellectual or scientific enquiry was ultimately, for her, a religious exercise:

> To see the harmony which subsists in the revolution of the heavenly bodies simply stated, and silently to mark how light and darkness, subsiding as we proceed, enables us to view the fair forms of things, calms the mind by cultivating latent seeds of order and taste. We trace in this manner, the footsteps of the Creator, and a kind of elevated humility draws us to the pure source of goodness and perfection, for all knowledge rises into importance, as it unites itself to morality. Morality or religion, for we use them as synonymous terms, is the soul of all . . . (vii, p. 142)

Wollstonecraft's high expectations of education frequently lead her into discussions of philosophy and psychology. One of the most important issues of the day, which occupies her in a number of reviews, was that of 'natural morality': that is, how far are human beings guided in the development of virtue by their own natural instincts in that direction? In a review (May 1789) of a work on the subject, Wollstonecraft finds herself entirely in agreement with the author's view that man's 'instinctive perceptions, [and] quick sense of right' prove that he is born with a latent moral sense which, when developed into 'finer shades' by the cultivation of reason, is the foundation of morality and virtue.

It is important, however, to distinguish between the instinct for right, possessed by human beings alone, and the lower instincts which

man shares with the animals. The failure to make this distinction is
the source of Wollstonecraft's dissatisfaction with William Smellie's
Philosophy of Natural History, which she reviews in October 1790. She
lends her unqualified approval to those parts of the work in which
Smellie gives accurate descriptions of the distinguishing characteristics and physical functions of human beings, animals, plants and
minerals, but objects strongly to his view that 'instinct is only a lesser
degree of reason' (vii, p. 295), and wonders whether 'in his ardour to
prove that animals have minds similar to the human intellect, he
meant to deprive us of souls' (vii, p. 296). For Wollstonecraft,
Smellie's belief that animals have mental capacities resembling those
of humans is easily disproved by a consideration of human
perfectibility – not only of the individual but also of the race as a
whole:

> If in the earlier stages of society, human architecture was extremely
> rude – that is inferior to the first essays of the beaver, bee, etc. it is
> natural to infer that reason and instinct are essentially different. The
> human species, considered collectively, appear to have an infancy,
> youth, etc. – Has anything similar ever been observed in the brute
> creation? (vii, p. 297)

Animals are clearly incapable of that development of virtue through
reason which is the prerogative of man. They cannot practise self-
denial or moderate their natural appetites; their artifices are the effects
of blind impulses; their docility is the effect of the 'strong passion' of
fear. Wollstonecraft pours scorn on Smellie's theory that man's
superiority consists solely in the fact that his mind is endowed with
a greater number of instincts, and that the 'noble faculty of reason' is
merely the '*wavering*' between these instincts (vii, p. 298):

> If reason, thought, or mind, is not something distinct from instincts
> or senses, what power compares the information they convey to us? Is
> wavering, or deliberating, – mind? (vii, p. 299)

Such 'straying into metaphysical labyrinths' (*ibid.*) clearly has strong
attractions for Wollstonecraft. By far the longest discussion in her
review of Macaulay's *Letters on Education* is given over not to
Macaulay's educational theories but to the philosophical essays at the
end of the work. She feels that Macaulay's essay on the origin of evil
is insufficiently precise: owing to her 'eagerness to defend revelation',

she has implied that the notion of the unlimited power of God is weakened by a suggestion that it is directed by wisdom; whereas for Wollstonecraft, 'no contradiction is implied by saying, that he *can* only do what his wisdom points out as best' (vii, p. 318). She feels that she herself is less confined by Christian orthodoxy than Macaulay, since she argues that a belief in immortality existed before the promulgation of the Gospel, and can still exist independently of a belief in revelation: 'God may be reverenced, as perfectly good and benevolent, by those who do not call themselves believers' (vii, p. 319). Finally, her discussion of Macaulay's 'very judicious conclusion to a book on education' – a defence of the doctrine of moral necessity, which holds that human actions are determined by all the foregoing circumstances of environment and education, and that man's belief that he has freedom of choice between good and evil is an illusion – indicates that while she agrees with Macaulay's reasoning in principle, she is prepared to take a more pragmatic view of the subject than she believes many philosophers are capable of:

> The virtuous Free-Willer still continues to cultivate his mind with as much care, that he may discern good from evil, and choose accordingly, as if he believed that the understanding was *quite* independent of the will; and in the education of his children he labours to fix good principles and habits, that every incitement of appetite may not lead the will astray. . . . The vicious necessitarian, on the other hand, suffers himself to grow as vain when he is flattered, and as angry when he is injured, as if his views were more confined: – and after neglecting his children, seems as much surprised at their disobedience, as he could be if he believed that good motives had no effect on the will . . . (vii, p. 321)

Politics

Godwin's *Memoirs* describes how the French Revolution produced:

> a conspicuous effect in the progress of Mary's reflections. The prejudices of her early years suffered a vehement concussion. Her respect for establishments was undermined. (Holmes (1987) p. 229)

This change is clearly reflected in her reviewing for the *Analytical*. Political issues are scarcely mentioned in her early reviews. Although she does note, in a discussion of *Sketches of Society and Manners in Portugal* (1788), that the comparative lack of civilisation in Portugal may be attributed to 'a religion most absurd, and a government most arbitrary' (vii, p. 29), she appears to give almost equal weight to the climate, the 'want of rational employments, and a mixture of Moorish customs' (vii, p. 31). Only in December 1790 does she begin to discuss political issues openly: it cannot be a coincidence that this was also the month in which she published her *Vindication of the Rights of Men*. It is probable, indeed, that her engagement with Burke led Johnson to begin to pass books which dealt with political issues to her to review.

In December 1790, Wollstonecraft reviews Helen Maria Williams's *Letters on the French Revolution, written in France, in the Summer of 1790 . . .* – a work which she would attempt, unsuccessfully, to emulate two years later in her unfinished 'Series of Letters on the Present Character of the French Nation'. She had reviewed Williams's *Julia* earlier in the year, and this work, which she finds interesting and unaffected, confirms her favourable opinion of 'the goodness of the writer's heart' (vii, p. 322). Wollstonecraft's wholehearted belief, at this stage, in the positive value of the Revolution is clear. She expresses the hope that Williams's sincerity may help to eradicate 'a *few* of the childish prejudices that have the *insignia* of raw-head and bloody-bones to sink them deeper in the vacant mind' (*ibid.*); asserts that 'the destruction of the Bastille was an event that affected every heart' (vii, p. 323); and quotes with approval passages which reflect badly on 'the late French government' (*ibid.*). A month later, in a heavily ironic review of *Lindor and Adelaide, a Moral Tale* (the work of Edward Sayer, a follower of Burke), she describes recent events in France as an 'exertion of reason to meliorate the wretched state of the poor', and deplores the fact that in Sayer's work the 'enormities' of the late government are 'thrown into the background by the old plea of necessity and trite remarks on the imperfection found in all human plans' (vii, pp. 343–4).

She is enthusiastic about David Ramsay's *History of the American Revolution*, an account of the war written by an American which she reviews in July 1791. Oddly, she charges him with using some 'awkward, unauthorized expressions', although presumably one of the reasons the war was fought was to free the natives from the tyranny of the King's English. But she finds his history entirely captivating – 'the narration assumes a romantic cast' – and she recommends the book to the young with ill-concealed breathlessness, giving the whole war a classical status:

> Young people will find this a valuable work, and the heart that glowed at the recital of Leonidas's struggle, will pantingly follow General Washington's march. (vii, p. 378)

The American Revolution, she says, has:

> interested the heart and exercised the understanding of every man, who is sufficiently enlightened to rise above the sensible horizon viewed by shortsighted selfishness, to the contemplation of the rational one, dimly discerned by reason. . . . The time is now arrived when not only the calm philosophical inquirer, but even *the true born Englishman* . . . will rejoice that freedom, and all its concomitant blessings, have been the reward of a glorious struggle, though the towering head of our proud isle has been stripped of some of its waving honours. The American revolution seems to form a new epoch in the history of mankind; for amidst the various changes, that have convulsed our globe, it stands forth as the first work of reason, and boasts of producing a legitimate constitution, deliberately framed, instead of being, like all other governments, the spurious offspring of chance. (vii, p. 375)

Her reaction indicates something of the illusion that liberals of the time shared regarding the French Revolution. They did not envisage the nature of the civil war in France, or the tyranny of the commune that replaced the monarchy – they expected it to follow the pattern set in America, which in any case, being a long way off, was easy to romanticise. France was different, and near enough to visit, and once she had experienced it Wollstonecraft shed her illusions. But the romanticism that still surrounded her view of America may well have made her more than usually vulnerable to Imlay when she met him. He seemed, at least at first, to embody all her expectations of America and the Americans – she described him in a letter as:

> A most worthy man, who joins to uncommon tenderness of heart and quickness of feeling, a soundness of understanding, and reasonableness of temper, rarely to be met with – Having also been brought up in the interior parts of America, he is a most natural, unaffected creature. (Wardle (1979) p. 251)

Her enthusiasm for America is reiterated in a review (September

1791) of Jean-Pierre Brissot's *Nouveau Voyage dans les États-Unis*, where she describes America as 'a country where his favourite theories received life by being introduced into practice'. Despite her warning about the 'colouring' that Brissot's experience of despotism in France may have persuaded him to throw over his view of America, she appears to share his warmth, and particularly notices the differences between American and European manners. She is impressed by his account of religious toleration, but even more so by the 'innocent frankness' of American women, which allows the sexes to converse in a friendly way, without 'gallantry and coquetry'. This she takes to be a clear proof of the 'purity of morals' prevailing in America:

> Men and women mix together like social beings; and, respecting the marriage vow, mutually improve their understandings by discussing subjects that interest the whole race; whilst in Europe the conversations that pass between *gentlemen* and *ladies*, in general, consist of idle compliments and lively sallies; – the frothy food of vanity. (vii, p. 391)

Brissot finds what he is looking for in America, and she follows him and finds what she is looking for in his book: honesty, frankness, toleration, simplicity of heart, goodness and naturalness – every virtue not commonly found in Europe because of the corruption of the governments and the repression of society by despotism. She believed in a utopian virtue, which is a credit to the kindness of her heart but shows, perhaps, little understanding of the nature of reality. In this she resembled other radicals of the day, who found what they wanted to find in America, hoped for it in France, and worked hard for it at home, not without some success, something achieved in the face of experience. Brissot was, of course, executed along with the other Girondists, and thus became a victim of the revolution he helped to shape.

Wollstonecraft's review of Brissot gives the first indication of an increasing preoccupation of hers: the fact that the lack of morals among the French people threatens to prove a stumbling block in the way of their future development – a problem which would be magnified for her when she observed them at first hand. In January 1792 she expresses the hope that the Revolution will in time have an effect on morals, which it must do unless it is 'but a phosphoric burst produced by levity, and not a noble glow of patriotism produced by reason': a citizen will no longer need to be educated to guard against debauchery, since 'the constitution and laws will educate him' by themselves (vii, p. 413–14). A month later she is attributing to the 'iron mace of despotism' the fact that the French national character has been pervaded by a 'fondness for intrigue', and blaming the idleness of the nobility for the 'kind of *gentlemanly* sensuality, that rendered their taste vicious, and ever at war with nature' (vii, p. 418). It is clear that at this stage she is accepting without question every rumour and cliché of radical rhetoric – in her review of *Mémoires of the Maréchal Duc de Richelieu* (vii, p. 383) she writes that the reign of Louis XIV laid the foundation of the despotism, depravity and repression, the destruction of 'all national equality and personal distinctions', which justified the Revolution. The root of the 'evil', she says, lies in depravity, orgy and perverted sexuality – a wholly puritan series of connections which she would reiterate in her *Historical and Moral View* two years later.

Although Wollstonecraft never openly expresses the hope – which would, in any case, have been dangerously radical even for the *Analytical* – that events in America and France might be the forerunners of a similar revolution in England, it is clear that she finds deplorable injustices and inequalities in her own country. In a long footnote to her review of Macaulay's *Letters on Education* she writes indignantly of the conditions prevailing in the public hospitals, where 'the poor are shamefully left a prey to the ignorant and the uninterested': the meat they are given to eat is often putrid and unwholesome; the patients are forced to pawn their few possessions to provide themselves with clean linen and are charged for the washing of their sheets; the cleaners, in their zeal to put everything in order for the charity committee, make 'the most infernal noise' in the wards where 'some poor neglected wretches [are] breathing their last' (vii, pp. 316–17). A review written in June 1792 expresses 'honest indignation' over the practice of removing poor children from their homes and putting them to work in the cotton mills of Manchester:

> Mistaken, indeed . . . must be principles of that commercial system, whose wheels are oiled by infant sweat, and supine the government that allows any body of men to enrich themselves by preying on the vitals, physical and moral, of the rising generation! – These things ought to be considered. (vii, p. 442)

In another review, written in the same month, she expresses doubts about the wisdom and usefulness of solitary imprisonment: it cannot, she feels, have any permanent effect on the prisoner's reformation. In this she anticipates both Coleridge ('The Dungeon') and Wordsworth ('The Convict') in the 1798 *Lyrical Ballads*: Wordsworth's poem deplores the effects of solitary confinement, and argues in favour of transportation as an alternative; while Coleridge's, which originally appeared in his tragedy *Osorio*, argues that in such circumstances:

> His energies roll back upon his heart,
> And stagnate and corrupt; till changed to poison,
> They break out on him, like a loathsome plague-spot . . .
>
> (ll. 8–10)

Wollstonecraft suggests that the prisoner might instead be taught a trade, then gradually allowed to work and to accumulate the profit as savings which he could use to establish himself in the world at the end of his sentence. This 'second education' would enable him to be given a testimony to the effect that he had 'redeemed his character, by acquiring a habit of industry' (vii, p. 422). Finally, there are several instances in the reviews, as elsewhere in Wollstonecraft's writings, where she shows that she was strongly opposed to the 'infamous traffic' (vii, p. 392) of the slave trade. She is particularly concerned about the conditions endured by the slaves both on board ship and in the West Indies, which 'make the blood turn its course' (vii, p. 100); and she speaks indignantly of 'the misery those poor wretches endure who languish in slavery, and the cruelty and injustice practised to entrap men' (vii, p. 282).

It is noticeable that in the years – from June 1788 to May 1797 – in which Wollstonecraft reviewed, she came to place rather less weight on reason and rather more on feeling and affection as she became more exposed to, and more deeply entangled in, the world of her emotions. She continued to respond more readily, more impatiently or more sympathetically to some ideas than to others, though she became more confident in handling abstract ideas and conceptual arguments. But she had also matured into a considerable author in her own right, although she continued to contribute reviews. Her last reviews appeared in May 1797, after her marriage to Godwin and within three months of the birth of Mary and her own death.

The *Analytical* ceased publication in December 1798, just over a year later. *The Anti-Jacobin Review*, which published an attack on

Johnson's subversive activities in the autumn of that year, stressed
the fact that the *Analytical* had begun at the very time when political
agitation started in France, and suggested that its inception had been
part of an orchestrated campaign, headed by Johnson, aimed at the
overthrow of the government.[5] In February 1799 Johnson was
sentenced to six months in the King's Bench Prison, despite being
represented by Thomas Erskine, who had so successfully defended
Thomas Holcroft and others against the charge of treason in 1794.
Johnson was charged with selling Gilbert Wakefield's pamphlet *A
Reply to Some Parts of the Bishop of Llandaff's Address to the People of
Great Britain*, which was actually published by J. Cuthell at the
beginning of 1798 and declared a seditious libel. There is no record
of the trial itself, but sentencing was – for unknown reasons –
postponed, and a testimony to Johnson's character as person and
bookseller was presented. At that hearing one further piece of
evidence was produced against Johnson: a copy of the *Analytical* for
September 1798, presumably as an indictment of his social attitudes
and political convictions, since no particular part of the journal was
indicated in any way – it was felt that a copy of the *Analytical* alone
was quite enough to convict him. The Attorney General was
determined to convict Johnson as an example to other Jacobin
printers: opinion had moved decisively against liberals and radicals;
and besides, juries were packed to ensure a verdict in accordance with
the Attorney General's wishes.[6]

The *Analytical*'s cessation in December was a direct consequence
of these events. The *Anti-Jacobin*, launched in November 1797 and
edited by William Gifford, was directed specifically against all liberal
tendencies, but particularly against those who might be tempted to
support ideas sympathetic to the French Revolution. The magazine
took credit for killing off the *Analytical*:

> the *Analytical Review*, has received its death-blow, and we have more
> reason to congratulate ourselves upon the share which we have had in
> producing its dissolution, than it would be expedient here to unfold.
> ('Prefatory Address to the Reader', *The Anti-Jacobin Review*, I, iv–v)

By this time Thomas Christie, its first editor, was also dead, and
members of the original Johnson circle – Priestley, Paine, Barlow,
among others – had dispersed.

While the *Anti-Jacobin* had little difficulty in ilustrating that the reviewers in the *Analytical* represented liberal rather than conservative points of view, nevertheless the *Analytical* was not, and never had been, an organ of opinion in which writers had the freedom to argue, debate, and express their attitudes towards social and political problems. The politics of the *Analytical* were more implicit than explicit. This, in fact, was the original purpose of the journal, and from the outset the reviewers' remit was severely limited by its function. Christie saw the journal's function as being to act as a filter, an indicator of good writing for the benefit of those in the professions, or others who held positions of influence in society, who were unable to find the time to read and make their own choices among so many published works. It was aimed at those:

> who, though they may have an ardent love of knowledge, and might be extremely useful in diffusing it, and promoting the benefits derived from it, are, however, too much involved in the necessary duties of their stations, to find leisure to peruse volumes in quarto and folio. (Nichols (1812–15) ix, pp. 384–6)

It was essentially a guide to good and interesting reading selected from available titles, and far from the organ of radical politics depicted by the *Anti-Jacobin*.

Chapter 3

◆

A Vindication of the Rights of Men (1790)

On 1 November 1790, Edmund Burke's *Reflections on the Revolution in France, and on the Proceedings in Certain Societies in London Relative to that Event: in a Letter Intended to Have Been Sent to a Gentleman in Paris* was published. His contemporaries were startled by the views expressed in it. Even Charles Depont, the 'Gentleman in Paris' to whom it was addressed, was stunned by the ideas it contained, and wrote in his *Answer to the Reflections of the Right Hon Edmund Burke* (London, 1791) that Burke was mistaken about much that had happened and was happening in France. He suggested that *Reflections* would strengthen the forces of reaction and counter-revolution, and asserted:

> I would not have hazarded my question had I been aware what effect it would produce, and [that] if your opinions had been known to me, far from encouraging you to disclose them, I should have intreated you to withhold them from the public. (p. 3)

First and foremost, Burke's friends and contemporaries were surprised that Burke should have condemned the Revolution so soon after the fall of the Bastille, and shocked that he should have reneged on his former friends and reversed the arguments that he had rehearsed in defending the American War of Independence: in his *Speech on Conciliation with America* (1775), for instance, he had defended the 'fierce spirit of Liberty' (p. 16), which had led the colonists to rise up against their oppressors.

Reflections was provoked initially by a sermon preached by Richard Price on 4 November 1789 to the members of the Revolution Society, who met each year to celebrate the anniversary of the Glorious Revolution of 1688. Burke assumed that Price's sermon, published as *A Discourse on the Love of Our Country* (1789), was directed at undermining the constitution, particularly in so far as he had affirmed liberty of conscience, the right to resist the abuse of power, and the right of a nation to choose its own governors, to cashier them for misconduct, and to frame a government for itself – all principles established, Price argued, in the overthrow of the 'rightful' king James II and the election of William III. Price had ended with an enthusiastic welcome to the present time as highly favourable to the cause of liberty, and a eulogy of the recent events in France, the millenarian optimism of which had provoked a letter of congratulation to Price from the newly elected French National Assembly. Although they were extreme, Price's views were not unrepresentative of the positive response which greeted the early days of the French Revolution. Burke's *Reflections*, however, attacked religious toleration and assumed that dissenters such as Price were enemies of the constitution. He presented the Revolution as a catastrophic event which was rapidly destroying the order of civilisation itself. He defended the *ancien régime* and argued for its total preservation – despite its long enmity towards Britain in over a hundred years of intermittent conflict, and despite his private view of it, expressed the following year, as 'that system of Court Intrigue miscalled a Government'.[1]

On its publication, Burke's pamphlet was an immediate commercial success, but he was grotesquely represented by the cartoonists and pilloried by the pamphleteers. He found few defenders. His defence of the Catholic clergy, contrasting with his persecution of English dissenters, aroused strong antipathy. His detractors recognised from the outset that Burke's real target was not France but Britain and the enemy within: the radicals and the dissenters were, he feared, grouping and reorganising to overthrow the king and plunge the country violently into an anarchy similar to that about to overtake France. His contemporaries were also surprised by the vehemence of Burke's attack and the emotionalism deployed in his arguments. They realised that the force of his intellectual analysis and discussion was generated by powerful, obscure and, they felt, personal feelings. Although later readers allowed Burke a certain prescience in seeing, while others had not seen, that the Revolution would lead to tyranny and terror, his later reactions to continuing activity by an alliance of Foxite Whigs and the English radicals makes clear his conviction that Britain would entirely go the way of France.

Of the numerous replies to Burke which were written, Wollstonecraft's *A Vindication of the Rights of Men, in a Letter to the Right Honourable Edmund Burke* was one of the first to be published. Godwin gives Wollstonecraft's own account of the composition: the manuscript sheets were apparently being sent to the printer as they were composed, when Wollstonecraft was 'seized with a temporary fit of torpor and indolence, and began to repent of her undertaking'. Johnson, instead of encouraging her to go on, told her he would gladly abandon the project, at which Wollstonecraft, her pride 'piqued', went straight home and finished the work (Holmes (1987) p. 230). The first edition appeared anonymously on 29 November 1790. A second edition, with additions and revisions chiefly aimed at sharpening the political arguments, and with Wollstonecraft's name on the title page, appeared three weeks later, on 18 December.

It does not seem impossible that Wollstonecraft's 'torpor and indolence' may have been partly a result of a realisation of her own audacity in replying to so exalted a personage as Burke, who had been a reformer for thirty years, a man feared and admired, whose personal views commanded attention and respect. Her reasons for pursuing the project were, presumably, both personal and political. Richard Price was a friend of long standing, and Wollstonecraft loved and admired him as a man and as a thinker. She had learnt much of her radicalism from him. As a minister he combined democratic principles with Christian morality, a combination of which she approved. She had written a highly favourable review of his *Discourse* for the *Analytical Review* in December 1789 (vii, pp. 185–7), in which she had quoted with approval passages which summarise most of what she herself stood for: his plea for wider educational opportunities; his demand for the repeal of the Test Act, and for reform of the franchise to make the House of Commons more representative of the people; and his eulogistic conclusion, which represented the tide of ignorance and despotism receding and being replaced by enlightenment and liberty.

But the *Rights of Men* is far from being simply an indignant defence of Price, although that forms a part of it. Wollstonecraft also takes the opportunity to air what appear to be long-standing disagreements with some of Burke's other writings, most notably his early work on the psychology of aesthetics, *A Philosophical Inquiry into the Origin of our Ideas of the Sublime and Beautiful* (1757). Crucially (and in this she differs from any of Burke's other respondents), she sees that the gender issues which were already present in Burke's aesthetic treatise are perpetuated by the sexual politics at the heart of *Reflections*.[2] A controversial episode in which Burke had recently been involved, the debates over the Regency Bill 1789, is also called in to help her score points against him.

In addition, Wollstonecraft doubtless knew that Catherine Macaulay had gained a good deal of fame from her pamphlet attacking Burke in 1770 (*Observations on a Pamphlet, entitled, Thoughts on the Present Discontents*). She knew and approved of Macaulay as a writer and as a woman, and knew she would do her own reputation no harm by taking on Burke. After all, Wollstonecraft had a name and a living to make, and she seized the chance to gain prominence in leading the attack on Burke. She knew that the radicals for whom Price spoke would support her. She had Joseph Johnson's agreement to publish the book on the hottest topic of the moment. But the haste of composition shows clearly. It is instructive to compare her response with that of Catherine Macaulay, whose reply to Burke's pamphlet, *Observations on the Reflections of the Right Hon. Edmund Burke, on the Revolution in France, In a Letter to the Right Hon. Earl of Stanhope* (London, 1790) was published shortly after Wollstonecraft's own. Macaulay, a trained historian and an experienced writer, is cool and detached; her argument is structured, and proceeds gradually and logically towards conclusions that are totally destructive of Burke's position. She is highly intellectual, she organises her material, and she knows what she is going to say before she says it.

Wollstonecraft, on the other hand, is impassioned and almost wholly unstructured. There is much in Burke's pamphlet which she ignores completely, probably because her energy and enthusiasm run out before she has dealt with it. Macaulay always meets Burke on his own ground, and defeats him there; Wollstonecraft is continually trying to force Burke on to her ground in order to fight him – in particular, by introducing her own views on men's tyranny over women, a subject which appears only by implication in *Reflections*. Nevertheless, Wollstonecraft's pamphlet has a passion, a force of language and style, which makes it readable and enjoyable in a way that Macaulay's, for all its obvious virtues, is not: it has been justly described as functioning 'as a poem rather than an argument' (Paulson (1983) p. 80).

Indeed, the liveliness of Wollstonecraft's pamphlet is largely attributable to the fact that she writes partly as an excuse to settle old scores, partly to air her own opinions, and only marginally to reply in any reasoned way to Burke. The only portions of the *Rights of Men* in which she does attempt a logical response to Burke's arguments are those where she sets out to defend Price, and Price's views, from Burke's attacks.

The disagreement between Burke and Price depends mainly on an interpretation of the principles established by the Revolution of 1688. It was an unavoidable fact that in that year a rightful king had been overthrown by the will of the people, and that in placing the succession on William III after Mary's death the hereditary principle had been made to give way to certain social and religious pressures. Not only must Burke have known this, but the Whig Party, to which he belonged, had made these principles the foundation of their policies throughout the century. He could not, however, afford to defend the overthrow of a monarch if he wished to attack Price. Thus he was forced to argue that the purpose of the Revolution had been to defend the '*antient* constitution of government . . . We wished . . . and do now wish, to derive all that we possess as an *inheritance from our forefathers*' (Burke (1989) p. 81). Wollstonecraft is obviously well aware of the fundamental issues at stake, and replies to Burke by reiterating Price's arguments, which take their origin from Locke's *Two Treatises of Government* (1689):

> there are rights which men inherit at their birth, as rational creatures, who were raised above the brute creation by their improvable faculties; and . . . in receiving these, not from their forefathers but, from God, prescription can never undermine natural rights. (v, p. 14)

She pours scorn on his appeals to the '*antient* constitution', pointing out that this, if it existed at all, was 'settled in the dark days of ignorance':

> Are we to seek for the rights of men in the ages when a few marks were the only penalty imposed for the life of a man, and death for death when the property of the rich was touched? when – I blush to discover the depravity of our nature – when a deer was killed? (v, p. 13).

She offers an alternative view of the 'birthright of man'; it is:

> such a degree of liberty, social and religious, as is compatible with the liberty of every other individual with whom he is united in a social compact, and the continued existence of that compact. (v, p. 9)

While it is clear that Wollstonecraft's defence of Price is partly based on her firmly held belief in his political ideals, her deep affection and respect for Price, a friend since 1783–4, is most apparent when she confronts what is personal, as opposed to political, in Burke's attacks. Burke had represented Price as confused and irresponsible, describing him as 'chant[ing] his prophetic song', making 'delusive, gypsy predictions', using 'the confused jargon of Babylonian pulpits', and moving the address to the National Assembly when 'the fumes of his oracular tripod were not entirely evaporated' (Burke (1989) p. 117). Wollstonecraft contrasts Price's 'modest virtues' and his 'piety and reason' – which, in spite of her unwillingness to 'look up with vulgar awe', nevertheless command her respect – with Burke's excessive praise of Marie Antoinette:

> I saw her just above the horizon, decorating and cheering the elevated sphere she just began to move in, – glittering like the morning-star, full of life, and splendor and joy. Oh! what a revolution! and what a heart must I have, to contemplate without emotion that elevation and that fall! . . . little did I dream that I should have lived to see such disasters fallen upon her in a nation of gallant men, in a nation of men of honour, and of cavaliers. I thought ten thousand swords must have leaped from their scabbards to avenge even a look that threatened her with insult. – But the age of chivalry is gone. (Burke (1989) pp. 126–7)

It is clear from this much-discussed passage that Burke had been captivated by the queen's youth, glitter and splendour; and, as many replies to Burke alleged, that charm appeared to be of greater importance to him than virtue. Wollstonecraft offers her readers an alternative portrait – one of Price himself, drawn, as Burke's had been, from memory:

> I could almost fancy that I now see this respectable old man, in his pulpit, with hands clasped, and eyes devoutly fixed, praying with all the simple energy of unaffected piety; or, when more erect, inculcating the dignity of virtue, and enforcing the doctrines his life adorns; benevolence animated each feature, and persuasion attuned his accents . . . (v, pp. 18–19)

While Burke's 'glittering' queen is purely decorative, Wollstone-craft's 'respectable' Price demonstrates that external appearance is of value only for the moral qualities which it represents. It is significant, however, that Wollstonecraft, despite her desire to defend Price, is willing to concede to Burke the point that perhaps 'Dr Price's zeal may have carried him further than sound reason can justify'; and that it may be difficult to see the future good which may result from 'present calamities' (v, p. 18).

Essentially, Wollstonecraft argues that Burke's attack on Price is based on a misrepresentation of his meaning, and that the indignation which Burke expresses over Price's closing ejaculation ('I may say, *Lord, now lettest thou thy servant depart in peace, for mine eyes have seen thy salvation* . . .' (Price (1798) p. 49) is an 'affectation of holy fervour' (v, p. 25). Indeed she views much of *Reflections*, from its rhetoric to its attitudes, as hypocritical. She points out that at the beginning of the previous year (February 1789) Burke had made a series of speeches in the House of Commons on the reading of Pitt's Regency Bill, which expressed views of monarchy that were entirely inconsistent with those he had put forward in the *Reflections*. This episode had gained a good deal of public notoriety for Burke, and Wollstonecraft was clearly conversant with much of the detail which was, in any case, public knowledge. In return for the offer of a post as Paymaster General, Burke had supported the Prince of Wales in his election to the Regency in November 1788, when George III had been declared insane. He had collected statistics from mental institutions to show the unlikelihood of the king's recovery, and had argued forcefully against Pitt's Regency Bill, which sought to limit the prince's powers. Most notably, throughout the debates on the Regency Bill, Burke had consistently attacked those provisions in the Bill that gave authority to the queen: for the care of her husband, for the royal household, and for the control of the Civil List money.[3] The violent rhetoric of his speeches on this occasion had led many to suggest that he was losing his reason. Cries of 'Take down his words' from the government side had greeted the moment (recalled as blasphemous by Wollstonecraft) in his speech of Monday 9 February 1789, when he had said:

> Ought they to make a mockery of him, putting a crown of thorns on his head, a reed in his hand, and dressing him in a raiment of purple, to cry 'Hail! King of the British'?[4]

Earlier in the same speech he had spoken of George III being 'smitten by the hand of Omnipotence, and . . . hurled . . . from his throne' by God; in *Reflections*, as Wollstonecraft notices, he uses the same phrase with a very different connotation: 'when kings are hurl'd from their thrones by the Supreme Director of this great drama . . . our minds . . . are purified by terror and pity' (Burke (1989) pp. 131–2). He had also argued in the Commons against giving an allowance to the queen on the grounds that it would create a fund for bribing Members of Parliament. Wollstonecraft points to the inconsistency of the fact that Burke had no scruples then about attacking the king and queen of England – who were surely as harmless as (and the queen, in her view, a good deal more virtuous than) the French monarchs – while now he is quick to defend the king and queen of France, and uses this fact to question his own sanity: 'Where then was the infallibility of that extolled instinct which rises above reason? was it warped by vanity, or *hurled* from its throne by self interest?' (v, p. 27).

Although the arguments of the *Rights of Men* are apparently tangential to a strict scheme of replying to Burke point by point, there is in fact an organising principle behind Wollstonecraft's thinking. Essentially, she uses *Reflections* as a starting point from which to air her general disagreement with Burke and everything he had come to stand for: conservatism as opposed to democracy, tradition as opposed to innovation, society as opposed to the individual, patriarchy as opposed to feminism.

The clash between Burke's conservatism and Wollstonecraft's radicalism is demonstrated by (among other issues) their opposing views of what she describes as 'the demon of property' (v, p. 9). While Burke's arguments rested on the value of heredity in upholding traditional values, Wollstonecraft suggests that hereditary property has, in fact, stopped the progress of civilisation by turning men into 'artificial monster[s]' who cannot exist without the homage paid to them as a result of their station in life (v, p. 10). She suggests that Burke's 'servile reverence for antiquity' would logically militate against the possibility of abolishing the slave trade (v, p. 14). She argues, with some justification, that 'it is only the property of the rich that is secure': the working man has no property to defend, though he loses his liberty – and often his life – when he is pressed into service in wars from which he has nothing to gain (v, p.15). She takes Burke's argument for the perpetuation of property in landed families, and suggests that this desire has, on the contrary, led parents to treat their children like slaves, sacrificing the younger ones to the eldest son, and putting a bar against early marriages which injures both the minds and the bodies of young men by producing 'lax morals and depraved affections' (v, p. 23). Furthermore, property spreads discontent among the middle classes, who are led to ape the manners of the great, and sacrifice domestic comfort to the 'destructive mildew' of the pursuit of it (*ibid.*). Wollstonecraft sees the Church, too, eulogised by Burke as an institution which demonstrates the sacredness of traditional values, as fundamentally corrupt, having secured 'vast property' in the past by exacting tithes and indulgences from the poor and ignorant (v, p. 39).

Property, she suggests, should be 'fluctuating': that is, it should be equally divided between all the children in a family (v, p. 24). The natural sanction for security of property should be only a man's right to whatever he has acquired by his own efforts, and he should be able to bequeath this to whomsoever he desires (v, p. 23). She believes that if property were to be properly redistributed, it could form the root of all happiness and virtue: she suggests that estates could be divided into small farms, and forests and common land given over to the poor; this, she thinks, would solve simultaneously the problems of lack of work, poor health and poverty (v, p. 57).

It is interesting to compare Wollstonecraft's ideas on property with those of Godwin, who wrote about it at length in *Political Justice*. In the first edition (1793) Godwin argues that property is a positive evil, and he, like Wollstonecraft, sees hereditary property not only as causing robbery and war but also as fostering vice, envy, malice and revenge. In an ideal society, private property would no longer exist; instead, any article of property would belong to 'him who most wants it, or to whom the possession of it will be most beneficial' (Godwin (1793) p. 135). In this view, Wollstonecraft's more liberalised plan for the redistribution of property to the poor would simply perpetuate the evil. Interestingly, by the second edition (1796) Godwin has revised many of his most extreme views, and argues that we do, in fact, have a right to property (see Philp (1986) pp. 134–8).

Wordsworth, on the other hand, although he was apparently a Godwinian for a short period after the publication of *Political Justice*, demonstrates in the poetry of the *Lyrical Ballads* (1798, 1800) that he, like Wollstonecraft, places a high value on the property ownership of the small farmer and also, at the time, shared her belief in the evils

accruing from the landed gentry – the very class that Burke defends
so aggressively. In 'The Female Vagrant' (started c.1795, and thus
the earliest poem in the *Lyrical Ballads*), for example, the vagrant's
father lives happily possessed of 'One field, a flock, and what the
neighbouring flood/Supplied' (ll. 3–4) until the 'greedy wish' of the
master of the 'mansion proud' dispossesses him of his 'old hereditary
nook' (ll. 39–44). In *The Last of the Flock*, written in 1798,
Wordsworth was, by his own account, illustrating his disagreement
with Godwin's view of property ownership:

> The man who holds with Godwin that property is the cause of every
> vice and the source of all the misery of the poor is naturally astonished
> to find that this so-called evil, the offspring of human institutions, is a
> vigorous instinct closely interwoven with the noblest feelings. It
> represents familiar and dearly loved fields, a hereditary cottage, and
> flocks every animal of which has its own name.[5]

Similarly, in 'The Brothers' and 'Michael' (both in the second volume
of *Lyrical Ballads*), as Wordsworth explained in a letter to Charles
James Fox in 1801, he was attempting to illustrate the 'inconceivable'
power of the 'domestic affections' which, he argues, are generated in
the 'statesmen' (or smallholders) by the proprietorship of 'small
estates, which have descended to them from their ancestors'
(Wordsworth (1967) p. 314). Here he appears to be in complete
agreement with Wollstonecraft, who writes eulogistically of the
domestic life of the 'industrious peasant', in which 'the cow that
supported the children grazed near the hut and the cheerful poultry
were fed by the chubby babes' (v, p. 57).

In the *Rights of Men*, there are further parallels with Wordsworth's
democratic project of foregrounding the situation of those in '[l]ow
and rustic life' (Wordsworth (1991) p. 245). Notwithstanding her own
bourgeois origins, Wollstonecraft's democratic principles are outraged by Burke's obvious contempt for the labouring classes. She
quotes as 'contemptible, hard-hearted sophistry' (v, p. 55) a passage
which demonstrates, for her, that Burke reveres hereditary property
and despises the poor:

> the people, without being servile, must be tractable and obedient.
> . . . The body of the people must not find the principle of natural
> subordination by art rooted out of their minds. They *must* respect that
> property of which they cannot partake. They must labour to obtain
> what by labour can be obtained; and when they find, as they commonly

do, the success disproportionate to the endeavour, they must be taught
their consolation in the final proportions of eternal justice. (Burke
(1989) p. 290)

Burke's reference to 'the swinish multitude' is notorious, and caused
howls of outrage from his detractors. Wollstonecraft's response is to
bring the argument round to the plight of the poor and the need for
law reform. She points out that the laws of the land are such that the
poor are suffering manifold injustices. Capital punishment can be
imposed for the theft of a few pounds. Able-bodied men can be press-
ganged into the armed forces; this not only deprives them of their
personal liberty but also causes hardship to the families who depended
on their industry (v, p. 15). Moreover, the effects of this 'despotic
practice' will be felt throughout society, since the poor, lacking a
proper training for their minds, will not be able quickly to throw off
the bad habits of thinking they will have acquired during their
military service:

> Pressing them entirely unhinges their minds; they . . . cannot return
> to their old occupations with their former readiness; consequently they
> fall into idleness, drunkenness, and the whole train of vices which you
> stigmatise as gross. (v, p. 17)

She points out the unfairness of the game laws, which allow a farmer
to plant 'decoy fields' to lure game next to the property of poor
smallholders, but forbid the smallholder, on pain of fine or
imprisonment, to kill the game which is devouring his crops (v,
p. 17). In cities, changing fashions frequently lead to mechanics being
laid off for want of trade: oppression makes man into 'a being scarcely
above the brutes . . . a broken spirit, worn-out body, and all those
gross vices which the example of the rich, rudely copied, could
produce' (v, p. 58). Although these arguments may appear tangential
to the central core of Burke's pamphlet, their presence in the *Rights
of Men* is justified as a defence of the class most closely involved in
perpetrating the Revolution in France for which, as Wollstonecraft
astutely observes, Burke demonstrates a complete lack of sympathy.
Here, as elsewhere in her pamphlet, Wollstonecraft is less interested
in answering Burke's arguments point by point than in tracking down
the underlying attitudes which she believes those arguments
represent.

She does the same thing again in another, related area of concern:

in her pamphlet, gender issues become associated with those of class. For example, she judges with particular harshness the important passage in which Burke describes the events of 5–6 October 1789, when the king and queen were taken from Versailles to Paris by a mob of what he calls 'the vilest of women' (Burke (1989) p. 165). As has recently been pointed out, in Burke's account these women, whom he describes as conducting the royal family to an accompaniment of 'horrid yells, and shrilling screams, and frantic dances, and infamous contumelies, and all the unutterable abominations of the furies of hell' (Burke (1989) pp. 164–5), have abandoned their femininity and come to epitomise all that he fears and mistrusts in the new order: to use his own aesthetic terminology, beauty (represented by the French queen and the *ancien régime*) has given way to terror (see Furniss (1991) *passim*).

Wollstonecraft neatly foregrounds the inflated rhetoric of Burke's description with the succinct pragmatism and social realism of her comment: '". . . the vilest of women." Probably you mean women who gained a livelihood by selling vegetables or fish, who never had any advantages of education' (v, p. 30). Burke's pity, she asserts, is reserved for 'the downfall of queens, whose rank alters the nature of folly and throws a graceful veil over vices that degrade humanity' (v, p. 15). Interestingly, however, Wollstonecraft's feminism in this instance overrides her class consciousness, so that she, unlike many of the other respondents to *Reflections*, does not dwell on Marie Antoinette's supposed lack of virtue. Instead, she makes the point that the queen of France, in common with anyone of her background, deserves pity for the 'almost insuperable obstacles' which have stood in the way of her acquisition of 'true dignity of character' (v, p. 30).

Towards the end of the *Rights of Men*, Wollstonecraft manages once again to bring her arguments round to the subject of the sexual politics of Burke's writings. A rumour is current, she says, that there are certain 'fair ladies, whom . . . the captive negroes curse in the agony of bodily pain, for the unheard of tortures they invent' (v, pp. 44–5). These ladies, she speculates with conscious irony, may perhaps have read Burke's *Philosophical Inquiry into the Origin of our Ideas of the Sublime and Beautiful*:

> You may have convinced them that *littleness* and *weakness* are the very essence of beauty; and that the Supreme Being, in giving women beauty in the most supereminent degree, seemed to command them,

by the powerful voice of Nature, not to cultivate the moral virtues that might chance to excite respect, and interfere with the pleasing sensations they were created to inspire. . . . Never, they might repeat after you, was any man, much less a woman, rendered amiable by the force of those exalted qualities, fortitude, justice, wisdom, and truth . . . if virtue has any other foundation than worldly utility, you have clearly proved that one half of the human species, at least, have not souls. (v, p. 45)

Clearly, these ladies have found their way into the *Rights of Men* as an excuse for Wollstonecraft to air particular grievances against Burke's aesthetic treatise, which she judges, with some justification, to be laced with misogyny. She is alluding directly to passages such as the one in Part 3 Section IX, where Burke argues that:

[beauty] in the female sex, almost always carries with it an idea of weakness and imperfection. Women are very sensible of this; for which reason, they learn to lisp, to totter in their walk, to counterfeit weakness, and even sickness. In all this, they are guided by nature. Beauty in distress is much the most affecting beauty. (Burke (1987) p. 110)

In the next section Burke goes on to argue that 'Those virtues which cause admiration, and are of the sublimer kind, produce terror rather than love. Such as fortitude, justice, wisdom and the like' (*ibid.*). Wollstonecraft sees clearly that these arguments are reinforcing gender stereotypes; she points out that if virtue could also come to be viewed as beautiful, men's taste could be transformed from sensual depravity to more 'manly' and rational feelings – a transformation which, she suggests, 'may be equally natural', while morally it would be far preferable. But, she continues:

Such a glorious change can only be produced by liberty. Inequality of rank must ever impede the growth of virtue, by vitiating the mind that submits or domineers . . . (v, p. 46)

These arguments are, in essence, precisely those which form the basis of her next work, *Vindication of the Rights of Woman*.

It is worth noting that Burke's private opinions, as expressed in his letters in the years following the publication of *Reflections* and the *Vindication of the Rights of Men*, fully support Wollstonecraft's impression of his misogyny. Although in January 1791 (two months after *Reflections* was published, and a month after the appearance of the *Rights of Men*) Burke was asserting that he 'really had not read any of [the replies to *Reflections*], though they have all been sent to my house' (Burke (1967) vi, p. 214), his letters in subsequent years suggest a profound antipathy to any women who challenged traditional roles or spoke out about their repression. In a letter to Mrs John Crewe, written in August 1795, he described Marie Roland (who had been guillotined in 1793) with chilling heartlessness as a 'bold, intriguing, female Regicide', and grouped her name with – among others – that of Wollstonecraft, whom he represented as having undermined the sanctity of the family, corrupted the young, and unleashed the evils of unprincipled and opportunist attacks on the very foundations of the state:

> I hope and supplicate, that all provident and virtuous Wives and Mothers of families, will employ all the just influence they possess over their Husbands and Children, to save themselves and their families from the ruin that the Mesdames de Staals, and the Mesdames Rolands, and the Mesdames de Sillery, and the Mrs Helen Maria Williams, and the Mrs Woolstencrofts [*sic*] &c, &c, &c &c &c and all that Clan of desperate, Wicked, and mischievously ingenious Women, who have brought, or are likely to bring Ruin and shame upon all those that listen to them. You ought to make their very names odious to your Children. The Sex has much influence. Let the honest and prudent save us from the Evils with which we are menaced by the daring, the restless and the unprincipled. (Burke (1967) viii, p. 304)

In the *Rights of Men* Wollstonecraft does not really answer Burke in any consistent way. She avoids many of the issues he raises, especially the principle of heredity and the flimsy basis for the rights of anyone but kings and aristocrats. She finds that all is not well in contemporary society, but there is little analysis of constitutional government – either on behalf of democracy, or to counter Burke's assumptions of hereditary rights. She shows herself to be an effective journalist arguing to persuade by rhetoric rather than a serious exponent of constitutional or political government. But she is effective, and her points strike home. Her rhetoric is powerful and her images are impassioned, especially where her heart is most strongly engaged – on behalf of women, the poor, the victims of oppression or of bad and cruel laws, for example.

The *Rights of Men* is damaging to Burke in its sincerity, its sense of authenticity, its sense of convictions deeply felt. It was, essentially, hack work for Wollstonecraft, a response to an opportunity, and she possibly did not realise the full significance of the ideological conflict she had entered. But it was of considerable importance in her life for two reasons: it gave her self-confidence, because it was the first time she had begun to express herself fully in her writings; and it made her famous – or notorious, depending on one's political stance – as a writer on the radical side. The reviewer in the conservative *Gentleman's Magazine* wrote that in his opinion the *Rights of Men* would 'poison and inflame the minds of the lower class of his Majesty's subjects to violate their subordination and obedience'. He also commented sneeringly: 'we were always taught to suppose that the *rights of woman* were the proper theme for the female sex.'[6] A few months later, Wollstonecraft appears to have come to the same conclusion.

Chapter 4

◆

Vindication of the Rights of Woman (1792)

Godwin says that the composition of the *Rights of Woman* 'was begun, carried on, and finished . . . in a period of no more than six weeks' (Holmes (1987) p. 232), but this does not seem to be entirely accurate. Wollstonecraft's letters show that she had started writing it before 6 October 1791, when she described it to William Roscoe, the Liverpool lawyer and a relatively new friend, as 'a book that I am now writing, in which *I* myself . . . shall certainly appear, head and heart –' (Wardle (1979) p. 203). As a second letter to Roscoe, on 3 January 1792, states: 'I shall give the last sheet to the printer today' (Wardle (1979) p. 205), it appears that Godwin's six weeks must be extended to at least thirteen. Even so, Wollstonecraft obviously felt that she had composed with undue haste: in this second letter she told Roscoe that she was dissatisfied with herself for 'not having done justice to the subject . . . had I allowed myself more time I could have written a better book in every sense of the word' (Wardle (1979) p. 205). She had the opportunity to make some improvements when the book went into its second edition. Most of these were cosmetic, but a few, especially those in the Introduction, had the effect of laying a stronger emphasis on the equality of the sexes. Wollstonecraft also added a paragraph to the Dedication to Talleyrand (whom she had met between the publication of the two editions) which strikes a more confident and personal note.

Gary Kelly has suggested that the *Rights of Woman* was written, in part at least, as a result of Wollstonecraft's desire to impress Henry

Fuseli, with whom by this time she was hopelessly in love (Kelly (1992) p. 106). Although this suggestion may appear somewhat diminishing, it should not be dismissed out of hand. Fuseli's influence on Wollstonecraft at this period should not be underestimated. Today he is chiefly remembered as the painter of the extraordinary 'Nightmare', which was exhibited at the Royal Academy in 1782 and rapidly became one of the most notable European icons of its age.[1] But Fuseli's contemporaries saw him as one of the finest minds of his generation. Admired in England by (among others) Cowper, Blake, Hazlitt and Leigh Hunt, and in Switzerland and Germany by Lavater, Herder, Zimmerman and Goethe – he had met the leaders of Germany's *Sturm und Drang* in Berlin in 1763, and had therefore experienced German Romanticism at first hand – he was widely regarded as an exponent and follower of Rousseau, whom he had met in Paris in 1766, and on whose life and work he had published an anonymous pamphlet in 1767, *Remarks on the Writings and Conduct of J.J. Rousseau.*

Wollstonecraft evidently came to know Fuseli through Johnson shortly after her move to London in 1788. This was the year in which Fuseli published his translation of his close friend J.C. Lavater's *Aphorisms on Man*. Shortly afterwards, Fuseli seems to have started work on his own book of aphorisms, which remained unpublished until after his death. Fuseli's biographer quotes several of his aphorisms on women:

> In an age of luxury women have taste, decide and dictate; for in an age of luxury woman aspires to the function of man, and man slides into the offices of woman. The epoch of eunuchs was ever the epoch of viragoes.
>
> Female affection is ever in proportion to the impression of superiority in the object. Woman fondles, pities, despises and forgets what is below her; she values, bears and wrangles with her equal; she adores what is above her. (Knowles (1831) iii, p. 144)

Brutally traditional, these are diametrically opposed to Wollstonecraft's views, and it seems not impossible that in writing her *Rights of Woman*, she was attempting, in part at least, to answer Fuseli.

In addition, it is certainly tempting to see both the strict puritanism and the confusion which the *Rights of Woman* displays in the presence of sexuality as arising from Wollstonecraft's circumstances and state of mind at the time of composition. Godwin says that Wollstonecraft 'saw Mr Fuseli frequently; he amused, delighted and instructed her' (Holmes (1987) p. 234). Indeed, he must have been a whole finishing school so far as she was concerned, and his pre-eminence, learning and creative genius certainly seemed even more brilliant to her, coming as she did from a largely provincial background. They were obviously intimate over a long period during which time she matured intellectually and aesthetically, and she was directly affected by his views on most things – apart from his views on women, which were clearly anathema to her, although not sufficiently loathsome to prevent her proposing a permanent alliance with him. She was obviously not put off by his coarseness or his improper conversation – it is not clear whether she knew of his sexual proclivities, though his obvious experience and maturity were possibly an added attraction. Despite his diminutive stature, his relatively advanced age, and his marriage, Wollstonecraft came to feel that she could not live without him: 'I find I cannot live without the satisfaction of seeing him and conversing with him daily'.[2]

Although Fuseli may have encouraged her at first, he clearly became increasingly irritated by her growing attachment. Wollstonecraft persuaded herself that her feelings for him were strictly non-sexual; indeed, it was on this basis that after the *Rights of Woman* was published, in August 1792, she unsuccessfully proposed a Platonic *ménage à trois* with him and his wife. Her subsequent relationship with Imlay – in which, as Godwin puts it, 'for the first time in her life, she gave loose to all the sensibilities of her nature' (Holmes (1987) p. 243) – clearly demonstrates – as, indeed, does her later attachment to Godwin himself – that she was happy, relaxed and fulfilled in a fully physical relationship. The effort to believe that her feelings for Fuseli were purely Platonic must have been considerable, and must have involved strong suppression of her natural sexuality. They also, it seems certain, contributed to the repressive puritanism of the work which she composed during this period.

The *Rights of Woman* is Wollstonecraft's best-known and most celebrated work. If she had not written it, it is unlikely that she would be remembered as anything more than a minor literary figure. Its existence has assured her a considerable, though not unmixed, reputation. The work itself has become a cornerstone of feminist thought, and is generally considered to be the first feminist manifesto. Without wishing to detract in any way from the power and originality of Wollstonecraft's achievement, it must be acknowledged that many of her arguments in the *Rights of Woman* had been put forward by earlier writers, although she was almost certainly not aware of the existence of many of them.

The debate on the relative equality of the sexes can, in fact, be traced back to an opposition which originated in classical Greece, between the Platonic and Aristotelian schools. In Chapter 15 of Plato's *Republic*, Socrates argues in favour of equality of educational opportunities for the female 'guardians'; he concludes that natural gifts are to be found here and there in both sexes, and that so far as her nature is concerned, woman is admissible to the same pursuits as man. Aristotle explicitly disagreed with this, and in his *Politics* he argues in favour of natural subordination. The Aristotelian view – supported by appeals to biblical authorities such as St Paul – dominated European culture during the Middle Ages; but with the coming of the Renaissance a revival of interest in Platonism led a number of writers to argue in favour of the recognition of female abilities. In France, Henri-Cornelius Agrippa published *La Supériorité du sexe féminin* in 1509 (translated as *Nobilitee and Excellencye of Woman Kynde* (1542)); in England Sir Thomas Elyot's *The Defence of Good Women* appeared in 1545.

In Britain, it was only in the second half of the seventeenth century that women themselves began to speak out on behalf of their sex. The most important woman writer of this period was undoubtedly Mary Astell. Astell's first book, *A Serious Proposal to the Ladies* (1694), was notable for its insistence that women had a right to a life of the mind, and its suggestion that all-female colleges could be founded to further women's opportunities for education. Like Wollstonecraft, Astell believed that lack of intellectual training was largely responsible for woman's secondary place in society. She encouraged her female readers to take themselves more seriously, and argued that they should learn to trust their own judgement. Astell's *Serious Proposal*, which had gone through five editions by 1701, produced an immediate impact on the women who read it. A number of important women writers clearly showed the influence of her thinking in their own work, among them Bathusa Makin, Elizabeth Elstob, Elizabeth Thomas, Lady Mary Chudleigh and Elizabeth Singer Rowe.[3]

It seems clear that the concentrated flowering of arguments for female liberty at this time owed much to the political climate. Indeed, it can be seen as an extension of the contemporary debate which had been set in motion by the publication of Robert Filmer's *Patriarcha* (1680), which claimed that paternal and political power were identical, rather than merely analogous. Written as a justification for the existence of an absolute monarchy, *Patriarcha* became a seminal work for the emergent Toryism of the period, as Locke's *Two Treatises of Government* (1690) became for the Whigs.[4] Interestingly, Mary Astell's political loyalties were firmly allied to the Tories, as were those of most of the women writers who followed her. It has been suggested that their own political persuasion made it particularly important for them to point out that their political opponents had failed to take women into account in their demands for freedom (Smith (1983) p. 10).

Despite the many obvious similarities between Mary Astell's arguments and Wollstonecraft's own, there is no indication that she had ever heard of – let alone read – the writings of Astell and her female contemporaries. This is not really surprising, since their works had been long out of print by Wollstonecraft's lifetime. She may, however, have read some of the male writers who were sufficiently impressed by Astell's *Serious Proposal* to incorporate some of its ideas into their own works. Defoe, in particular, acknowledged a debt to Astell's ideas on female education in his *An Essay upon Projects* (1697), where he argues that 'a woman well bred and well taught, furnished with additional accomplishments of knowledge and behaviour, is a creature *without comparison*' (p. 294). Defoe's *Roxana* (1724) contains powerful arguments in favour of female independence, and his *Conjugal Lewdness; or Matrimonial Whoredom* (1727) anticipates Wollstonecraft's use of the term 'legalized prostitution'. Wollstonecraft may also have encountered Richard Steele's *The Ladies Library* (1714), which incorporates a hundred pages of *A Serious Proposal* without, however, acknowledging their source (see Perry (1986) p. 100).

Arguments in favour of greater equality of education and opportunity for women continued to find occasional expression in the writing of male authors throughout the eighteenth century – most notably in Francis Hutcheson's *System of Moral Philosophy* (1755) and John Miller's *Origin of the Destruction of Ranks* (1771, revised 1779). But two pamphlets by the pseudonymous 'Sophia', *Woman Not Inferior to Man* (1739) and *Woman's Superior Excellence to Man* (1740), whose titles speak for themselves, were the only prose works written by women which offered an identifiably feminist argument; while a survey of *Eighteenth Century Women Poets: An Oxford Anthology* (ed. Roger Lonsdale, 1989) reveals a noticeable reduction in polemicism throughout the century. To some extent this must be attributable to the shift in emphasis from reason to feeling, or sensibility; even the so-called bluestockings of the second half of the century, although they moved in male-dominated literary circles, never argued in favour of more than improved educational opportunities for women.[5] For this reason, Wollstonecraft's sense that she was breaking new ground is understandable.

The woman writer to whom Wollstonecraft owed her greatest debt was undoubtedly Catherine Macaulay. Macaulay's *Letters on Education* – which, as her review in the *Analytical* makes plain, Wollstonecraft admired greatly – may have influenced her thinking when she came to write the *Rights of Woman*. Certainly there are passages in the work which anticipate some of the ideas in Wollstonecraft's book. For example, Macaulay argues that boys and girls should be educated together, and that girls should be allowed to play as freely as boys rather than having their natural vivacity suppressed, since physical weakness is at the root of 'most of the caprices, the teasing follies, and often the vices of women'; she refers, ironically, to Burke's eulogies on attractive female weakness in *On the Sublime*, just as Wollstonecraft does in the *Rights of Men* (Macaulay (1790) pp. 47–8). She speaks disparagingly of the notion that women are not capable of absorbing a classical education; this, she asserts, must derive from 'the notion of a positive inferiority in the intellectual powers of the human mind' (Macaulay (1790) p. 49), and she pleads with parents to cultivate the minds of their daughters, and to allow their children to be brought up together, so that 'both sexes will find, that friendship may be enjoyed by them without passion' (Macaulay (1790) pp. 49–50). In a later passage, which Wollstonecraft quoted approvingly in her *Analytical* review, Macaulay states:

> The situation and education of women . . . is precisely that which must necessarily corrupt and debilitate both the powers of mind and body. From a false notion of beauty and delicacy, their system of nerves is depraved before they come out of the nursery; and this kind of depravity has more influence over morals, than is commonly apprehended. But it would be well if such causes only acted towards the debasement of the sex; their moral education is, if possible, more absurd than their physical. The principles and nature of virtue, which

is never properly explained to boys, is kept quite a mystery to girls. They are told indeed, that they must abstain from those vices which are contrary to their personal happiness, or they will be regarded as criminals, both by God and man; but all the higher parts of rectitude, every thing that ennobles our being, and that renders us both innoxious and useful, is either not taught, or is taught in such a manner as to leave no proper impression on the mind . . . .Whilst we still retain the absurd notion of a sexual excellence, it will militate against the perfecting a plan of education for either sex. (Macaulay (1790) pp. 207–8)[6]

Certainly all these arguments may be found in the *Rights of Woman*, but to assert that Wollstonecraft took them from Macaulay would be to oversimplify. She speaks of herself as 'coinciding in opinion with Mrs Macaulay relative to many branches of education' (v, p. 175), and it seems more likely that she found in *Letters on Education* a confirmation of the thinking which had been taking shape in her own mind, and towards which she had been moving increasingly in her own writings. In addition, as she acknowledges herself in the *Rights of Woman*, Macaulay was a valuable role model, an 'example of intellectual acquirements supposed to be incompatible with the weakness of her sex . . . her judgement, the matured fruit of profound thinking, was a proof that a woman can acquire judgement in the full extent of the word' (*ibid.*). Although the educational arguments in Macaulay's work find echoes in the *Rights of Woman*, however, her writing here lacks the political dimension which, as the title makes clear, Wollstonecraft made a point of including.

On the other side of the Channel, feminism had played a much more prominent part in Enlightenment thought throughout the second half of the century. Arguments in favour of female equality may be found in Diderot's *Sur les Femmes* (1772) and Holbach's *Des Femmes* (1773). By the time of the Revolution, ideas were being put forward which strongly resembled the politically conscious polemicism of the *Rights of Woman*. In 1790, Condorcet published a short work, *Sur l'Admission des femmes au droit de cité*, which argued that to deprive women of the vote was a violation of natural rights, since women, as rational, sentient beings, had the same rights as men. If women appeared inferior to men in mental ability, he suggested, this was probably owing to their inferior education, which was also responsible for the fact that they obeyed their feelings rather than their consciences. He pointed out the unfairness of excluding them from their natural rights on the grounds that they lacked the knowledge of how to exercise them, since their ignorance was a result of lack of experience. He concluded by arguing that the more degraded women are by unfair laws, the more pernicious their influence will be, and that this would decrease if it ceased to be their sole means of defence. In 1791 the actress and feminist activist Olympe de Gouges (born Marie Gouze in 1748) published *Déclaration des droits des femmes et des citoyennes*, a pamphlet of seventeen *articles* which constituted itself as a reply to the *Déclaration des droits de l'homme*, which had excluded women from civil and political responsibilities. The *article* most often quoted is no. 10: 'La femme a le droit de monter sur l'échafaud, elle doit avoir également celui de monter à la tribune' ('Woman has the right to mount the scaffold; she should have the equal right to mount the platform'), a claim which becomes painfully ironic, since de Gouges herself was to be executed in 1793 without, needless to say, having attained the second right for which she argued so memorably.[7]

Wollstonecraft, who was not usually backward in acknowledging her admiration of authors whose ideas she approved of, gives no indication, in the *Rights of Woman* or elsewhere, that she had read Condorcet's or de Gouges's writings. It seems virtually impossible, given her obvious interest in the events taking place in France, that she would not at least have heard of their existence. It is particularly significant that de Gouges's *Déclaration* was published in September 1791 – precisely the time when the idea of writing the *Rights of Woman* must have been born. Claire Tomalin has suggested that Wollstone-craft may have encountered Condorcet's ideas through Thomas Paine. She points out that Wollstonecraft is known to have met Paine at Johnson's on 13 November 1791, and suggests that he 'dropped into [her] mind the idea of a book about women's rights' (Tomalin (1977) p. 102). Wollstonecraft had started writing the book by 6 October, some seven weeks before the famous dinner party (Wardle (1979) p. 203). She may, of course, have had earlier, unrecorded meetings with Paine during which the subject came up: Thomas Rickman, with whom Paine was living in London from July 1791 to September 1792, includes Wollstonecraft among those who visited and were visited by Paine in London at this period, and who 'were among the number of his friends' (Rickman (1819) pp. 100–1).

Although an awareness of the existence of radical feminist thought in Paris may well have contributed to Wollstonecraft's decision to write, however, the step from the *Rights of Men* to the *Rights of Woman* is not a very large one, and many of the ideas in the *Rights of Woman* are, in any case, anticipated in her earlier writings. In addition, as Wollstonecraft's own Dedication to the *Rights of Woman* makes clear, a contributory factor was her disappointment on finding that Talleyrand's *Rapport sur l'instruction publique* (Paris, 1791), while calling for free intellectual, physical and moral education for both sexes, stated that women's education should be directed towards their playing a subservient role.

As the title of the work suggests, the fact that the *Rights of Woman* was written in the aftermath of the French Revolution and at the height of Wollstonecraft's enthusiasm for revolutionary principles meant that its general tendency was radical and polemical. However, although Wollstonecraft's arguments do undoubtedly have a strong political cast, she is also concerned with other issues. Education, as always, is of fundamental importance in her thinking. She sees it as having a far-reaching influence on the perception, by men and women alike, of gender roles; and she also discusses the question of how it could be improved in the future. Another concern which reappears in this work is the association between reason and virtue or morality: as in her earlier writings, this is firmly predicated on her belief in the individual's responsibility to develop a right relationship with God. She discusses the relationship between the sexes: love, marriage, family life and parenthood. Finally, she outlines some of the changes, both individual and social, which she hopes may result from an adoption of the views she expresses.

Gender

The question of gender – that is, a socially constructed view of the 'feminine' as opposed to a biological difference of sex – is crucial to the argument of the *Rights of Woman*. Wollstonecraft begins by attempting to establish the fundamental premiss that so far as the ability to reason is concerned, there is no innate difference between the sexes. The first three chapters are devoted to a close examination of this view which, Wollstonecraft argues, although seemingly self-evident, is not recognised by society as a whole. She begins by returning once again to what she calls 'first principles': the fact that it is reason which separates mankind from the rest of the animal

kingdom; that mankind's highest attainment is virtue; that knowledge is to be gained through a struggle with the passions (v, p. 81).
Such improvement, she goes on to argue, is the benevolent intention
of God, instituted for the purpose of developing our immortal souls,
and rendering us 'capable of enjoying a more godlike portion of
happiness' (v, pp. 83–4). If it is accepted that women have souls, then
it follows that these principles apply equally to them. However,
arguments have frequently been advanced to demonstrate the theory
that women have not 'sufficient strength of mind to acquire what
really deserves the name of virtue' (v, p. 88). She points to several
instances, including Milton's depiction of Eve as wholly subservient
to Adam ('God is thy law, thou mine: to know no more/Is woman's
happiest knowledge and her praise' (*Paradise Lost*, Book iv, ll. 637–
8)) and Rousseau's recommendations that woman should not be
allowed any independence, and her primary lessons should be in
obedience (Rousseau (1974)). Throughout recorded history, man has
acted upon the premiss that woman was created for him: even if the
biblical account of the creation of Eve from one of Adam's ribs were
to be taken literally, all it proves, in Wollstonecraft's view, is that man
has 'from the remotest antiquity, found it convenient to exert his
strength to subjugate his companion' (v, p. 95). As a result, women
have been kept in a state of artificial ignorance, and required to be
virtuous simply in obedience to the dictates of men, rather than as a
result of their own reasoned perception of the value of virtue.
Wollstonecraft is refreshingly dismissive of such attitudes: 'What
nonsense!' (v, p. 94); 'How grossly do they insult us who thus advise
us to render ourselves gentle, domestic brutes!' (v, pp. 88–9):

> Strengthen the female mind by enlarging it, and there will be an end
> to blind obedience; but as blind obedience is ever sought for by power,
> tyrants and sensualists are in the right when they endeavour to keep
> women in the dark, because the former only want slaves, the latter a
> plaything. (v, p. 93)

Interestingly, she is prepared to concede that, since the female
constitution is less physically strong than the male, 'men seem to be
designed by Providence to attain a greater degree of virtue'; even so,
she argues that woman's possibility of attainment must be 'equal in
quality if not in degree' (v, p. 95).

In terms of their capacity for reason and their potential for self-
development, Wollstonecraft sees no fundamental difference between

the sexes, but she does not extend this lack of differentiation to all aspects of life. The area which is most problematic for her here is that of sexuality. In Chapter 5, discussing Rousseau's view that women should be kept under restraint because when they are allowed to indulge themselves they do so to excess, she draws a parallel with '[s]laves and mobs', who 'have always indulged themselves in the same excess when once they broke loose from authority. The bent bow recoils with violence, when the hand is suddenly relaxed which held it' (v, p. 152). At the time when the *Rights of Woman* was written, this would have been seen as a highly topical and extremely relevant comparison. Not only was she writing in full consciousness of the violence which had, almost from the beginning, accompanied the Revolution in France, but also – as the reference to slaves shows – she was thinking of the recent uprising in the French colony of St Domingue (August 1791), in which the slaves burned plantations and killed their masters. The uprising was seized on by the opponents of Abolition, and indeed by conservatives of all descriptions, as clear proof of the dangers inherent in the doctrine of 'rights' (see Wilson (1989) p. 74). But, as Cora Kaplan has pointed out, to draw a parallel between revolutionary violence and female sexuality is to tread on dangerous ground (Kaplan (1986) p. 44). Later in the *Rights of Woman* Wollstonecraft describes the behaviour of prostitutes, who, she says:

> trample on virgin bashfulness with a sort of bravado, and glorifying in their shame, become more audaciously lewd than men, however depraved, to whom this sexual quality has not been gratuitously granted, ever appear to be. (v, p. 192)

This point, which is intended to illustrate the difference between innate ignorance and acquired modesty, is difficult to reconcile with her (biologically essentialist?) argument that '[a]s a sex, women are more chaste than men', who are 'certainly more under the influence of their appetites than women' (v, pp. 194, 207). Cora Kaplan argues, with some justification, that the *Rights of Woman* recoils from sexuality, if only by emphasising the need for the virtue of modesty and the suppression of 'nasty or immodest habits' (v, p. 197) (Kaplan (1986) p. 41). In a sense, however, the problem goes deeper than she suggests, since in asserting that Wollstonecraft's analysis 'insists, with commendable vigour, that these filthy habits are a social construction, foisted on each generation of women by male-dominated and male-orientated society' (*ibid.*) Kaplan is ignoring the profound ambivalence demonstrated by the two opposing views of sexuality displayed by the passages quoted above. In other words, Wollstonecraft seems to be suggesting that whether they are more modest or more lewd, these traits are inborn, and not acquired as a result of social pressures.

Education

Although Wollstonecraft does appear to take the view that women do differ from men in some non-biological respects, most of the arguments in the *Rights of Woman* are intended to demonstrate that 'femininity' is a social construct. In her analysis, she comes close to an Althusserian model of the 'ideological state apparatus', in which the components of education, law, family pressures, literature and the arts reinforce cultural ideology, and are instrumental in constituting (women's) positioning of themselves within that ideology (see Althusser (1984)).

Not surprisingly, education becomes the focus of many of Wollstonecraft's arguments. She begins the *Rights of Woman* with an unequivocal statement: after careful consideration, she has concluded that 'the neglected education of my fellow creatures is the grand source of the misery I deplore' (v, p. 73). Indeed, she is concerned not only about neglect – a fault of omission – but also about the more active problem of a 'false system of education' (*ibid.*) which has been perpetrated by male writers, and has become the basis of the very fabric of society, dictating the way in which men and women perceive their roles, both as individuals and in relation to each other. She takes the term in its broadest sense, making the important point that '[m]en and women must be educated, in a great degree, by the opinions and manners of the society they live in' (v, p. 90). While men are educated in order that they may make their own way in the world, women's education has only one end in view:

> To rise in the world, and have the liberty of running from pleasure to pleasure, they must marry advantageously, and to this object their time is sacrificed, and their persons often legally prostituted. (v, p. 129)

She points out how easily the accepted female stereotype gets

reinforced by society, and by the 'educational' works given to girls to
read:

> Everything she sees or hears serves to fix impressions, call forth
> emotions, and associate ideas, that give a sexual character to the mind.
> . . . Besides, the books professedly written for her instruction all
> inculcate the same opinions. (v, p. 186)

The basis of Wollstonecraft's educational theory, here as elsewhere,
is the Lockean model of the association of ideas. She discusses this at
length in Chapter 6 ('The Effect which an Early Association of Ideas
Has upon the Character'), and describes what she calls the 'habitual
slavery' to first impressions which can take hold of a mind that is not
capable of tempering those associations by means of the intellect.
Women are more frequently a prey to these habits of association, she
argues, because, unlike men, they lack the opportunity to engage in
business and 'other dry employments of the understanding, [which]
deaden the feelings and break associations that do violence to reason'
(v, p. 186).

She describes what she sees as the purpose of a proper education,
asserting, as she has asserted before, that education must foster
independence of thought, since 'it is a farce to call any being virtuous
whose virtues do not result from the exercise of its own reason' (v, p.
90). She offers a more detailed analysis of the benefits of the kind of
education from which women are excluded: because their education
lacks order and system, women are deprived of the opportunity to
acquire habits of exactitude and method. Consequently, they come
to rely on a 'negligent kind of guesswork', and never learn the ability
to generalise on matters of fact (v, p. 91). A woman who has devoted
her time to intellectual pursuits will naturally be possessed of greater
dignity and 'purity of mind' (v, p. 193); the petty indolence and vanity
which are so frequently alleged to be an intrinsic part of women's
nature would disappear if women were given the opportunity to study
politics and morality (v, p. 241).

A chapter is devoted to the subject of national education. She
acknowledges a debt to Talleyrand's *Rapport sur l'instruction publique*
in her recommendation of the establishment of day schools, to be set
up and financed by the government, in which boys and girls could be
educated together (v, pp. 239–40). Coeducation, she argues, will
naturally lead to more rational relationships between the sexes:

> Mankind should all be educated after the same model, or the
> intercourse of the sexes will never deserve the name of fellowship, nor
> will women ever fulfil the peculiar duties of their sex, till they become
> enlightened citizens, till they become free by being enabled to earn
> their own subsistence, independent of men. . . . Nay, marriage will
> never be held sacred till women, by being brought up with men, are
> prepared to be their companions rather than their mistresses . . . (v,
> p. 237)

Although Wollstonecraft acknowledges, in this passage and elsewhere
in the work, that marriage and motherhood may be many women's
final destination, she expresses regret for the fact that 'women of a
superior cast have not a road open by which they can pursue more
extensive plans of usefulness and independence' (v, p. 217). She
makes the tentative suggestion – a radical one in an age when female
suffrage had never been seriously suggested – that women should have
representatives in Parliament, pointing out the unfairness of a system
which governs them arbitrarily without allowing them a voice (*ibid.*).
At the very least, she suggests that they could be allowed to study
medicine, and become nurses, midwives or doctors. Other suitable
pursuits might include the study of political theory or history. With
a proper education they could also go into business for themselves,
'which might save many from common and legal prostitution' (v,
p. 218).

Even should such grand schemes seem impossibly distant,
however, she argues that society will still benefit from the improvement of women's education, since 'unless the understanding of
woman be enlarged, and her character rendered more firm, by being
allowed to govern her own conduct, she will never have sufficient
sense or command of temper to manage her children properly' (v,
p. 223); in other words, only a properly educated woman will be
capable of producing children who will be useful members of society.

Wollstonecraft's view of education is a broad one, which includes
the idea that literature reinforces the way in which women constitute
themselves as subjects within their society. She devotes a long chapter
of the *Rights of Woman* to 'Animadversions on Some of the Writers
Who Have Rendered Women Objects of Pity Bordering on
Contempt'. The first – and longest – section discusses Rousseau's
Émile (1762, 1763), a work which had had a profound influence on
educational writers during the decades that followed its publication,
including most, if not all, of those subsequently considered in the

Rights of Woman. Like some mid-twentieth-century feminist writers, she frequently simply quotes Rousseau's own words, allowing them to stand as a form of self-condemnation without the need for further comment. Rousseau had argued that women's inferior physical strength meant that they were intended to be weak and passive, and to subject themselves to men: Wollstonecraft asserts that, at the risk of being accused of irreligion or even atheism, she doubts whether women were created for men, as she believes that such a view is 'derogatory to the character of the Supreme Being' (v, p. 148).

She quotes a long passage in which Rousseau describes the differences which he recommends between boys' and girls' education, based on his view that girls 'are from their earliest infancy fond of dress', and that they are fonder than boys of 'things to show and ornament; such as mirrors, trinkets, and dolls'. She points out that what he calls a 'primary propensity' is nothing of the kind – it is a result of social conditioning: 'they were treated like women, almost from their very birth' (v, p. 151).

Her analysis of Rousseau's theories astutely recognises that it is what she calls his 'sentimental lust' which colours his view of women. He depicts them as he would wish them to be in order to excite his passion most fully, and is opposed to giving them a rational education because they would cease to be the weak and defenceless creatures he finds so appealing:

> 'Educate women like men', says Rousseau, 'and the more they resemble our sex the less power they will have over us'. This is the very point I aim at. I do not wish them to have power over men; but over themselves. (v, p. 131)

Wollstonecraft criticises comparable tendencies in the writings of James Fordyce, whose *Sermons to Young Women* (1765) and *Character and Conduct of the Female Sex* (1776) followed Rousseau in emphasising women's weakness and frailty. She objects strongly to the 'lover-like phrases of pumped up passion, which are everywhere interspersed', and finds particularly distasteful a passage in which Fordyce describes the powerfully striking effect of the sight of a beautiful woman at prayer, on which she comments:

> Why are women to be thus bred up with a desire of conquest? the very word, used in this sense, gives me a sickly qualm! . . . Why are girls to be told that they resemble angels; but to sink them below women? . . .

> Yet they are told, at the same time, that they are only like angels when
> they are young and beautiful; consequently, it is their persons, not their
> virtues, that procure them this homage. (v, p. 164)

Dr John Gregory's *A Father's Legacy to his Daughters* (1774) is
criticised on a number of grounds. Like Rousseau, Gregory had
asserted that a fondness for dress was 'natural' to women – a term
which Wollstonecraft says she is unable to comprehend: 'If they told
us that in a pre-existent state the soul was fond of dress, and brought
this inclination with it into a new body, I should listen to them with
a half smile . . .' (v, p. 97). She is more troubled by his advice to girls
not to dance with spirit, for fear of exciting libertine desires in men
(*ibid.*); to wives to conceal the extent of their affection (v, p. 98); and
to women in general that they should keep any learning they may have
acquired a secret (v, pp. 167–8).

Although she has demonstrated at length the fact that women's
inadequate sense of themselves is a product of social conditioning,
unsatisfactory education, and misleading 'educational' works,
Wollstonecraft reserves special indignation for women writers who
'argue in the same track as men, and adopt the sentiments which
brutalize them' (v, p. 171). Earlier in the work she had quoted 'the
following ignoble comparison' from Anna Barbauld's 'To a Lady with
some Painted Flowers' ('Flowers, sweet, and gay, and delicate like
you. . . .') (v, p. 123 n.). In the fourth section of Chapter 5, she
criticises Hester Lynch Piozzi and Madame de Staël for agreeing with
the Rousseauesque sentiment that women's arts should be employed
for the sole purpose of gaining a man's heart (v, pp. 171–2), and
Madame de Genlis for recommending '*blind* submission to parents'
(v, p. 174).

Politics

Godwin's description of Wollstonecraft's purpose in writing the
Rights of Woman rightly emphasises the political aspect of her
argument:

> She considered herself as standing forth in defence of one half of the
> human species, labouring under a yoke which, through all the records
> of time, had degraded them from the station of rational beings, and
> almost sunk them to the level of the brutes. She saw indeed, that they

were often attempted to be held in silken fetters, and bribed into the
love of slavery; but the disguise and the treachery served only the more
fully to confirm her opposition. She regarded her sex . . . as 'In every
state the slave of man: the rich as alternately under the despotism of a
father, a brother and a husband; and the middling and poorer classes
shut out from the acquisition of bread with independence, when they
are not shut out from the very means of an industrious subsistence.
(Holmes (1987) p. 231)

Just as many twentieth-century feminist theorists see a relationship
– albeit a troubled one – between Marxism and feminism, so
Wollstonecraft too finds parallels between class and gender oppression. The foundation of her argument is that if women are admitted
to be rational, they have 'natural rights' equal to those enjoyed by
men. Clearly this suggests that men, by depriving women of those
rights, are subjecting them to unjust oppression. In her dedication to
Talleyrand she points out the unfairness of the fact that the newly
formed French Assembly has attempted to redress the balance as far
as class oppression is concerned, but has failed to do the same for
women. Their belief that they are acting in women's best interests in
doing so simply echoes the arguments of:

tyrants of every denomination, from the weak king to the weak father
of a family; they are all eager to crush reason, yet always assert that
they usurp its throne only to be useful. Do you not act a similar part
when you *force* all women, by denying them civil and political rights,
to remain immured in their families groping in the dark? (v, p. 67)

Elsewhere she points out the fallacy of the assertion that 'tyrannic
kings and venal ministers have used . . . that woman ought to be
subjected because she has always been so' (v, p. 114). She draws a
parallel with arguments – which, she says, she has heard even
intelligent people advance – in favour of retaining an aristocracy: that
the masses must be inferior, or they would rise up in protest at the
treatment they receive; whereas instead they seem happy to submit
to oppression and simply live for the moment. It is a measure of the
state of degradation to which women have been reduced, Wollstonecraft argues, that they have come to live only in the present, and 'at
last despise the freedom which they have not sufficient virtue to
struggle to attain' (v, p. 121). She makes the point that women are
enslaved to men not only in the sense that they are expected to serve

and obey them without question; they are also slaves 'in the political and civil sense' (v, p. 239): that is, they have no right to choose their governors or to control their own property, because the law makes 'an absurd unit of a man and wife'. In addition, they are 'made slaves to their persons', since they must make themselves alluring to ensure that they get themselves husbands who will 'guide their tottering steps aright' (v, p. 215). As these quotations show, much of the rhetoric of the *Rights of Woman* is predicated on the comparison of women to slaves and men to their masters. This is scarcely surprising, since during the first two years of the 1790s the topic was under constant discussion both inside and outside Parliament. A recent biographer of the tireless Abolitionist Thomas Clarkson points out that during the early months of 1790 'slavery was the topic of the day in drawing-rooms, pulpits and debating societies' (Wilson (1989) p. 61). Wollstonecraft would almost certainly have read Clarkson's *Essay on the Slavery and Commerce of the Human Species, particularly the African* (1786, reprinted several times) which concludes:

> Slavery is contrary to reason, justice, nature, the principles of law and government, the whole doctrine, in short, of natural religion, and the revealed voice of God. (p. 256)

As her frequent references to Burke's parliamentary speeches in the *Rights of Men* indicate, Wollstonecraft was a close follower of proceedings in the Houses of Parliament, and she would undoubtedly have read the published accounts of the debates on the slave trade, which began in May 1789 and were still taking place during the period when she was writing the *Rights of Woman*. The slavery issue, of course, was simply another facet of the debate which was raging at the time over the question of the rights of man in general. The Anti-Abolitionists argued that Africans were subhuman, and therefore not entitled to rights of any kind; hence Wilberforce's impassioned statement during the debate of 18 April 1791:

> I have already gained for the wretched Africans the recognition of their claim to the right of *human beings*, and I doubt not that the Parliament of Great Britain will no longer withhold from them the rights of *human nature*.[8]

Wollstonecraft was already a convinced Abolitionist by 1790, as her references to 'the infernal slave trade' ('this abominable mischief') (v, pp. 50, 51) in the *Rights of Men* and in her reviews ('that infamous traffic' (*Analytical Review*, 11 (September 1791): vii, p. 392)) make clear. As with the other political issues she raises in the *Rights of Woman*, only a small step is needed to apply the reasoning of the anti-slavery campaign to the issue of women's eligibility for human rights.

Despite the parallels which can be drawn, Wollstonecraft was not a proto-Marxist in any real sense of the term. She begins the *Rights of Woman* with a statement that she is going to pay 'particular attention to those in the middle class, because they appear in the most natural state' (v, p. 75). Although she argues in favour of abolishing – as the title of her ninth chapter puts it – 'the Unnatural Distinctions Established in Society', she is not, in fact, recommending a classless society. Her suggestions for national education allow for a common education for all only up to the age of nine, after which 'girls and boys, intended for domestic employments, or mechanical trades, ought to be removed to other schools, and receive education in some measure appropriated to the destination of each individual' (v, p. 240). Her picture of an ideal marriage has a woman 'discharging the duties of her station with perhaps merely a servant-maid to take off her hands the servile part of the household business' (v, p. 213). These moderate (some might say bourgeois) views are extended into her discussion of gender relations. Her remark that since the beginning of history woman 'has always been either a slave or a despot' (v, p. 123) illustrates the fact that although she sees a number of parallels between the condition of women and that of oppressed classes, she is also aware of other possible comparisons which broaden the political perspective of her argument. Anticipating possible objections to a one-sided view, she admits:

> I may be told that a number of women are not slaves in the marriage state. True, but they then become tyrants; for it is not rational freedom, but a lawless kind of power, resembling the authority exercised by the favourites of absolute monarchs, which they obtain by debasing means. (v, p. 226)

She repeats a point which she had made in the *Rights of Men*:

> It is impossible for any man . . . to acquire sufficient knowledge and strength of mind to discharge the duties of a king, entrusted with absolute power; how then must they be violated when his very elevation is an insuperable bar to the attainment of either wisdom or virtue, when

all the feelings of a man are stifled by flattery, and reflection stifled by
pleasure . . . for all power inebriates weak man. . . (v, p. 85)

In some respects Wollstonecraft views women in the same light as
kings, or the rich. Since they are put on a pedestal – as the prevailing
view of them as primarily ornamental means that they frequently are
– and denied access to the creative and educational struggles of daily
life, women's only recourse is 'enervating pleasure', which leads them
to neglect both their domestic duties and the more important pursuit
of virtue and morality (v, p. 133). Furthermore, the fact that they are
denied any access to public office means that they can acquire power
only indirectly, through cunning and manipulation, and so they are
'debased by their exertions to obtain illicit sway' (v, p. 239). She
provides an astute analysis of the hierarchy of power relations – even
if women fail to rule, either directly or indirectly, in the public sphere,
they will behave in the home like 'viceregents allowed to reign over
a small domain':

> It will not be difficult to prove that such delegates will act like men
> subjected by fear, and make their children and servants endure their
> tyrannical oppression. As they submit without reason, they will,
> having no fixed rules to square their conduct by, be kind, or cruel, just
> as the whim of the moment directs; and we ought not to wonder if
> sometimes, galled by their heavy yoke, they take a malignant pleasure
> in resting it on weaker shoulders. (v, pp. 116–17)

Elsewhere she draws a parallel between women and soldiers. Officers
are equally obsessed with their appearance, as devoted to dancing and
parties, and as dedicated to flirtation and 'gallantry' as women, and
for much the same reason: they have been sent into the world without
a proper education or an acquired sense of morality. Wollstonecraft
comments that it is unfair to censure women for having 'a passion for
a scarlet coat', since their education has 'placed them more on a level
with soldiers than any other class of men' (v, p. 93 and n.).

She also draws an important equation between financial and moral
independence. Hereditary property – which she had attacked in the
Rights of Men – is once again presented as the basis of many of the
'evils and vices which render this world such a dreary scene to the
contemplative mind' (v, p. 211). Hereditary wealth breeds idleness,
and society will never improve until this is abolished and man is
enabled to develop his faculties by exercising them. But true social

equality must include both sexes, or women, in their ignorance, will be constantly undermining it:

> It is vain to expect virtue from women until they are in some degree independent of men. . . . Whilst they are absolutely dependent on their husbands they will be cunning, mean, and selfish . . . (v, pp. 211–12)

Marriage

A consideration of the conditions and expectations of marriage is an important theme in the *Rights of Woman*. Once again, it is easy to suppose that Wollstonecraft's observations of Fuseli's marriage – to a pretty woman who was demonstrably his social and intellectual inferior – gave additional weight to her stringent views on the subject. In addition, another of her friends, Henry Gabell, had recently married, and she had been displeased by the physical displays of affection between him and his new wife: 'I think I could form an idea of more *elegant* felicity – where mind chastens sensation, and rational converse gave a little dignity to fondness' (Wardle (1979) p. 194).

In any case, for the vast majority of women marriage was the only viable alternative to poverty and the 'disgrace' of spinsterhood – a fact which produced, in Wollstonecraft's view, a most undesirable state of affairs. She thinks it degrading that women should be always 'subservient to love or lust' (v, p. 96), and unwise that they should have to rely for all their happiness on someone who is 'subject to like infirmities' (as weak, in other words) as themselves (v, p. 97). In addition, she deplores the kind of education – or lack of it – which the goal of marriage demands, in which:

> strength of body and mind are sacrificed to libertine notions of beauty, to the desire of establishing themselves – the only way women can rise in the world – by marriage. And this desire making mere animals of them, when they marry they act as such children may be expected to act – they dress, they paint, they nickname God's creatures. Surely these weak beings are only fit for a seraglio! Can they be expected to govern a family with judgement, or take care of the poor babes whom they bring into the world? (v, p. 76)

Quite apart from the damage which is done to a woman's capacity for moral or spiritual development by such a limited and oppressive upbringing, there are sound pragmatic reasons for deploring such a state of affairs. The so-called love – 'the most evanescent of all the passions' (v, p. 96) – which a man may feel for a weak, delicate, dependent creature must, by its very nature, diminish with the passing of time; without the affection and respect which can result only from a consciousness that the woman is his intellectual equal, the husband will rapidly lose interest in her when her beauty fades. Alternatively, she may be widowed, and left with a large family to bring up alone, which she will be wholly unequipped to do if she has never thought or acted for herself (v, p. 117); or, indeed, she may fail to find a husband at all. In any of these cases, if she has been deprived of the kind of education which would allow her to be strong and self-sufficient, she will be lost, both materially and morally.

Related to this line of argument is Wollstonecraft's attempt to undermine the concept of romantic love, which she presents as little more than an illusory and destructive fantasy. Once again, it seems clear that her stringent anti-romanticism is partly a result of her own troubled feelings. Indeed, she goes so far as to put forward the view that 'an unhappy marriage is often very advantageous to a family, and . . . the neglected wife is, in general, the best mother' (v, p. 99). Moreover, she suggests at one point – unpromisingly – that this state of affairs 'would almost always be the consequence if the female mind were more enlarged' – because, she sternly argues, what we gain in pleasure and enjoyment of the present moment must be correspondingly debited from any gains we might make in wisdom and progress towards virtue and knowledge (*ibid.*). To replace romantic love, she suggests that a successful marriage would be one in which 'the calm tenderness of friendship [and] the confidence of respect' (*ibid.*) formed the basis of the relationship. She looks forward to 'some future revolution in time', when women may have developed into the rational beings she wishes them to be, and foresees that 'even love would acquire more serious dignity' – women would cease to be attracted to men for spurious qualities like gallantry, and men to 'look for beauty and the simper of good humoured docility' (v, pp. 188–9). She envisages a companionate marriage, in which respect tempers the indulgence of the appetites, so that the couple are not united simply in order to gratify their physical desires:

> The feelings of a parent mingling with an instinct merely animal, give
> it dignity; and the man and woman often meeting on account of the

child, a mutual interest and affection is excited by the exercise of a common sympathy. (v, p. 208)

She realises that motherhood will continue to be the lot of most women, and sees this as yet another reason for arguing that they should receive a more comprehensive education. Even if they continue to be denied any power of their own in the world, their children will be the citizens of the future; thus both they and society as a whole will benefit from having mothers who are more rational and virtuous. The lack of female education at the present time leads to the fact that women seldom exert 'enlightened maternal affection'; instead they either neglect their children or spoil them by overindulgence (v, p. 222). Foolish, ignorant women cannot, by the nature of things, be expected to be good mothers. Wollstonecraft envisages a properly educated woman as being able to contribute in fundamental ways to her children's physical and mental well-being from the very beginning of life. She advocates breastfeeding – which 'wealth leads women to spurn' (v, p. 213) – not only because it is healthy but also because it provides a natural means of producing 'an interval between the birth of each child' (v, p. 263). Also, a husband whose heart is not absolutely cold will feel 'more delight at seeing his child suckled by its mother than the most artful wanton tricks could ever raise' (v, pp. 212–13).

One of Wollstonecraft's arguments for educating boys and girls together is that it would be 'a sure way to promote early marriages'. This she sees as desirable, as it would prevent the constitution of boys being 'ruined by . . . early debaucheries' (v, p. 240). If a man does indulge his appetites outside marriage, and seduces a woman:

> it should, I think, be termed a *left-handed* marriage, and the man should be *legally* obliged to maintain the woman and her children. . . . the woman who is faithful to the father of her children demands respect, and should not be treated like a prostitute . . . (v, pp. 139–40)

She argues forcefully, however, against the prevailing double standard which condemns prostitution. Frequently an innocent girl takes the first step in this direction as a result of seduction by an unscrupulous man, in which case her action cannot even be condemned as an error, as she has been duped by her own sincerity and affection for her seducer. Rejected by society, she can never 'recover her former station . . . no exertion can wash this stain away'.

Necessity forces her into prostitution, and the way of life which has been forced on her by circumstances quickly degrades her character. Wollstonecraft deplores the prevailing view that 'with chastity all is lost that is respectable in woman', and exclaims against the ethos of Richardson's *Clarissa*, in which the heroine, having been drugged into a state of unconsciousness before her rape by Lovelace, tells him that he has robbed her of her honour: 'miserable beyond all names of misery is the condition of a being who could be degraded without its own consent' (v, pp. 140–1). She appears not to be aware, incidentally, that this could be seen as inconsistent with the later passage in which she is less charitable about prostitutes, describing them as 'glorifying in their shame', and as having 'consign[ed] themselves to infamy' (v, p. 192). This has led at least one critic to suggest that her views on the subject are contradictory, and that in this passage she is holding women responsible for their own degradation (Reiss (1989) pp. 25–6). Her point, however, is that these 'audaciously lewd' women began life as 'bashful, shamefaced innocents' (terminology which echoes her earlier description) who lacked the steady virtue to enable them to withstand the societal pressures which have led to their present way of life: thus society, and an unsatisfactory education, are fundamentally to blame rather than the women themselves. As she puts it in a later chapter: 'make [women] free, and they will quickly become wise and virtuous' (v, p. 247).

Although Wollstonecraft sees male prejudice and male-dominated education as forming the basis of the inferior and oppressed condition of women, it is not to men alone that she addresses her argument. She sees clearly that if the changes which she advocates are to be effected, women must be made aware of the ways in which they are perpetrating the stereotype which has been imposed on them by men: 'it is your own conduct, O ye foolish women! which throws an odium on your sex' (v, p. 252). Her arguments, moreover, are directed beyond individual cases of either sex, and take in the social conditions and institutions which have propagated the attitudes she deplores. She is well aware that her recommendations would involve radically altering the very structure of society.

As a critic, Wollstonecraft always places more emphasis on description than on prescription; in other words, she is more concerned to show what is wrong with society than to recommend what should be put in its place. But she does include a number of suggestions for educational reform, and for extending the public and professional avenues open to women. In addition, she is more cautious than many of her contemporaries about participating in the post-revolutionary utopianism of the day. But the *Rights of Woman* is, without question, a fundamentally optimistic work. She declares in the first chapter: 'Rousseau exerts himself to prove that all *was* right originally: a crowd of authors that all *is* now right: and I, that all will *be* right' (v, p. 84). By the end, she hopes to have proved that society as a whole will benefit from an improvement in the moral status of women, since clearly no collection of individuals can approach the ideal if half its members are deficient in those qualities which would tend towards the general good: 'the most salutary effects tending to improve mankind might be expected from a REVO-LUTION in female manners . . .' (v, p. 265).

Vindication of the Rights of Woman brought Wollstonecraft instant literary celebrity. The work was favourably received on the whole, although its unashamedly radical politics naturally attracted its share of mockery and condemnation. Reviewers praised Wollstonecraft's sound emphasis on female education, and the values of marriage and motherhood. The harshest criticism came from *The Critical Review*, which called Wollstonecraft's reasoning 'vague' and 'inconclusive' and her style 'weak, diffuse, and confused'.[9]

Chapter 5

◆

'Letter Introductory to a Series of Letters on the Present Character of the French Nation' (1793/1798) An Historical and Moral View of the Origin and Progress of the French Revolution (1794)

Although a number of circumstances had contributed to Wollstone-craft's decision to move to France at the end of 1792, as a professional writer she certainly felt that an advantage would be gained by responding to the public demand for commentaries on the French Revolution written by English sympathisers *in situ*. Her first attempt, which was presumably intended to be published either in the *Analytical Review* or in some other journal, was the short piece which appeared in Godwin's posthumous edition of her unpublished works under the title 'Letter Introductory to a Series of Letters on the Present Character of the French Nation', dated 15 February 1793. Perhaps she was attempting in this to emulate the success of the radical writer and poet, Helen Maria Williams, who had been living in Paris since 1790 and had published a popular work on the French Revolution, *Letters Written in France in the Summer of 1790* (1790); a second volume had been added for the second edition of 1792, and a third had appeared in 1793[1].

The *Historical and Moral View*, of which Wollstonecraft managed to complete only the first of an unspecified number of projected volumes, was a much more ambitious work than the 'Series of Letters' had promised to become. Although again she was obviously responding to the popular demand for information about events across the Channel, she was also filling a gap in the market in the sense that her work was intended not only to give information but also to comment on it from the point of view of a supporter of the Revolution.

Thus no work of the exact nature of the *Historical and Moral View* had previously appeared. The newspapers reported events on a day-to-day basis, of course, and the *New Annual Register*'s Historical section published year-by-year accounts. Arthur Young's *Travels [in France] during the Years 1787, 1788, and 1789* (Bury St Edmunds, 1792) included lively and sympathetic comments on the Revolution (which Young retracted the following year in his pamphlet *The Example of France a Warning to Britain*). But apart from Helen Williams's works, which did not pretend to be comprehensive from an historical point of view, the only book-length study in English to have appeared before Wollstonecraft's was that of Thomas Christie – the co-founder, with Joseph Johnson, of the *Analytical Review* – whose *Letters on the Revolution in France* was published in 1791 as one of the replies to Burke's *Reflections*. British readers would also have had access to Henry Frederic Groenvalt's *Letters Containing an Account of the late revolution in France*, translated from German by Dumont and Romilly in 1792. Another work, J.P. Rabaut Saint Étienne's *Précis historique de la Révolution française*, which appeared in two volumes in France in 1792, does not seem to have found its way to England. In any case, neither of these works contained the kind of commentary and analysis which Wollstonecraft offered in the *Historical and Moral View*.

During the months immediately preceding Wollstonecraft's arrival in France in December 1792, the violence of the Revolution had escalated alarmingly. On 10 August 1792 the king had been deposed and imprisoned after a confrontation at the Tuileries between the National Guard and the king's Swiss guard in which 400 attackers and 800 defenders were said to have been killed, their mutilated bodies being burned on bonfires in the Place de la Carrousel – an event described by Robespierre as 'the most beautiful revolution that has ever honoured humanity' (Schama (1989) pp. 614–15). Later that month the guillotine was first set up in the Place de la Carrousel, and the revolutionary tribunal, established on 17 August, began the series of arrests, imprisonments and executions without trial which were to continue, and escalate, over the coming months: over one thousand people were arrested in the two weeks following the establishment of the tribunal alone. On 2 September began the 'September massacres', an event which, according to a recent historian, has 'no equal in atrocities committed during the French revolution by any party' (Schama (1989) p. 631). Over the four days which followed, over half the prisoners in Paris – at least fourteen hundred people – were executed in cold blood, without any kind of trial. On 22 September, France was proclaimed a republic. At the end of the following month Robespierre, who was fast emerging as the leader of the recently formed National Convention, was denounced as a would-be dictator by the moderate Louvet.

On 11 December, Louis XVI was indicted and accused of crimes against the state, and on 26 December he was put on trial. His fate was evidently a foregone conclusion, as Wollstonecraft perceived (see her letter to Johnson on 26 December, quoted below), and he was executed on 21 January 1793, less than a month after Wollstonecraft's arrival in Paris. Ten days later, on 1 February 1793, following the condemnation by the British government of the execution of the king, France declared war on England. The following months saw the purge of the leaders of the moderate Girondist party – many of whom Wollstonecraft is said to have met – the rise to power of Robespierre and the Jacobin party, and the subsequent Reign of Terror (October 1793–July 1794) in which, it has been claimed, as many as forty thousand people – the majority of whom were not aristocrats or nobility, and not connected in any way with the *ancien régime* – were executed, supposedly for treason (Schama (1989) p. 791 and *passim*). This was the context in which Wollstonecraft set out to write a positive and sympathetic account of the French Revolution.

Wollstonecraft had originally planned to travel to France in the summer of 1792 with Joseph Johnson, and Henry Fuseli and his wife. She was obviously planning in part to capitalise on the success of the *Vindication of the Rights of Woman*: as she wrote to her sister Everina on 20 June: 'I shall be introduced to many people, my book has been translated and praised in the popular prints' (Wardle (1979) p. 213). The party had got as far as Dover, but they changed their minds and turned back after hearing news of troubles in Paris. During the autumn, Wollstonecraft had found herself increasingly unhappy owing to the unrequited passion which she had developed for Fuseli, and she had decided to go to France on her own. She had arrived in Paris in the last week of December, and almost at once found herself unexpectedly in tears at the sight of Louis XVI being transported across Paris to his trial, 'sitting, with more dignity than I expected from his character, in a hackney coach going to meet death'. Later that day – 26 December – she wrote to Johnson that she was unable to sleep:

I cannot dismiss the lively images that have filled my imagination all
the day . . . once or twice, lifting my eyes from the paper, I have seen
eyes glare through a glass door opposite my chair, and bloody hands
shook at me. Not the distant sound of a footstep can I hear. . . . I want
to see something alive; death in so many frightful shapes has taken hold
of my fancy. (Wardle (1979) p. 227)

Her first instalment of a failed attempt to write her impressions of
Paris and the character of the French people, the 'Letter Introductory', was apparently written some six weeks later. In his *Memoirs*,
Godwin attributed her failure to continue with this project to the fact
that she had been temporarily depressed and lonely when she arrived
in Paris. He contended that the 'gloominess of her mind communi-
cated its own colour to the objects she saw', and 'tinged [her writing]
with the saturnine temper which at that time pervaded her mind'
(Holmes (1987) pp. 101, 102). However, the 'Letter Introductory'
reveals a more profound disturbance of mind than can be dismissed
as merely the result of a passing depression; Wollstonecraft seems to
have suffered a real failure of philosophical optimism.

The most striking thing about the 'Letter Introductory' is that
despite the fact that Wollstonecraft was writing for publication, and
that she was obviously expected by her publishers and readership to
write about the events in France with a sympathetic and positive
outlook – after all, she had greeted the Revolution with as much
optimism as anyone in her earlier works, and had travelled to Paris
partly because of her ardent support for its principles – she was unable
to refrain from expressing the most profound philosophical doubts.
The letter is a product of disenchantment (the new Jerusalem having
proved to be not at all what she had hoped for), tiredness, the result
of adjusting to a new language and environment – her French, at least
when spoken, was not as intelligible as she had hoped, and in any case
she was inhibited from using it at first – and loneliness, her isolation
emphasised by being abroad and away from familiar things. But her
disillusion with the Revolution is clear: she blames the French
character, which lacks the seriousness of the Anglo-Saxon. The
people are too frivolous, too fond of self-indulgence, too happy, to be
thoughtful or wise. They live, she thinks, on the surface of life, and
they lack the English habit of introspection. They are refined, urbane,
without being concerned with morality or ethics. The vices of
aristocracy have been replaced by the vulgarity of commercialism,
money replacing birth as the social criterion of class. The evils of the

old system have been replaced by the destruction and bloodshed of the new. The hoped-for vision, the brotherhood of man, the unbroken sovereignty of virtue, are mirages and dreams. Indeed, experience suggests that man is moved to action more readily by vice than by virtue, by evil than by goodness, driven onwards by self-indulgence, by vanity and by wishful thinking; and that disillusion is the only outcome. Helping others is doomed to disappointment and ingratitude.

The benefits of the Revolution, she thinks, will be felt in Paris later than elsewhere; none the less, the government seems to be encouraging selfishness, cold-heartedness and ignorance. There is a noticeable absence of humanity, sincerity and self-denial – those qualities supposedly repressed by despotism and released by the new dispensation. She sees this anarchy, vice, cold-heartedness and selfishness as characterising the new France. In government everything is as it was under the *ancien régime*: only the names are changed. The principles of government are the same: power for power's sake. She is the English moralist repeating many of the strictures against the French who did not enjoy inhibition, self-immolation and the constant moral anxieties in which puritan England has always wallowed. There is no doubt that Wollstonecraft's puritanism was shocked by their sexual attitudes, which she quickly interpreted as licentiousness: to her, a depraved aristocracy could only produce a depraved government, manners, sexual morals and economy being all of a piece. Her distrust of the French is centred on what she describes as 'their favorite epithet, amiable' (vi p. 443), derived from *aimer*, to love. They enjoy the 'refinements of sensuality' by stifling every 'moral emotion', thereby hardening their hearts. Wollstonecraft is in effect reviewing the French and expressing her disappointment at the quality of their lives, which she describes as superficial, and their enjoyment of life, which she finds immoral. Suspicious of gaiety, she, with her 'English head', looks for 'more solid happiness'.

Curiously, the only French people who measured up to Wollstonecraft's standards morally were the extreme Jacobins, especially Robespierre, who was – sexually, at least – entirely incorruptible. There is also the paradox that France's more liberal moral standards encouraged Wollstonecraft to embark on her affair with Imlay: she clearly recognised that whereas in France she could find wide acceptance as an unmarried mother, in England, outside a narrow circle, she would be condemned as a fallen woman and socially ostracised.

Certainly – and understandably – Wollstonecraft feels that democracy is not to be trusted in the hands of the French. She sees nothing of the Paris others saw: the centre of fashion, the society of manners, wit and philosophy envied by Europe, the vigorous life of the intelligence and the prominence given to art and the arts. The graciousness, the style, the urbanity which many felt to be so civilised (and civilising) in aristocratic France leave her cold. Her prejudice against social inequalities blinds her to other things. In any case, there is a strong streak of the solid, trade-based middle class in her make-up which gives her little patience with the niceties of high culture, since it depends so much on wealth and property. To her, leisure is merely a polite word for time-wasting and idleness, and the French alone, she says, 'understand the full import of the word leisure' (vi, p. 443). She is only too aware that the Devil finds work for those who have leisure, and the Devil's tools are just that sensuality and 'animal spirits' that the French have in such abundance.

Apart from her obvious disappointment in not finding in France, its people or its government, those qualities that she expected – more than hoped – to find in a nation standing at the dawn of a new enlightenment, her prose is tired, and at times it lacks her usual bright lucidity. Moreover, the letter is strangely devoid of those images, pictures, scenes, touches of speech or personal asides, domestic details or any kind of concrete picture that might bring the description to life. She rehearses a number of tired metaphors drawn from the common stock of her writing without introducing originality or freshness anywhere:

> I wish I could inform you that, out of the chaos of vices and follies, prejudices and virtues, rudely jumbled together, I saw the fair form of Liberty slowly rising, and Virtue expanding her wings to shelter all her children! I should then hear the account of the barbarities that have rent the bosom of France patiently, and bless the firm hand that lopt off the rotten limbs. (vi, p. 444)

It is particularly interesting to note, in this extract, the fact that Wollstonecraft's expectations and wishes, which are in obvious conflict with observable reality, are all expressed in literary clichés ('the fair form of Liberty', 'Virtue expanding her wings', 'the firm hand that lopt off the rotten limbs'). As she had written many times in the *Analytical Review*, inflated language fails to express genuine feeling. Despite her attempts to remind herself of the evils of the *ancien régime*, she is unable to confront with equanimity the continuing atrocities which she sees taking place around her. As a result, all her most fundamental beliefs are under threat:

> Before I came to France, I cherished, you know, an opinion, that strong virtues might exist with the polished manners produced by the progress of civilization; and I even anticipated the epoch, when, in the course of improvement, men would labour to become virtuous without being goaded on by misery. But now, the perspective of the golden age, fading before the attentive eye of observation, almost eludes my sight; and, losing thus in part my theory of a more perfect state, start not, my friend, if I bring forward an opinion, which at the first glance seems to be levelled against the existence of God! I am not become an Atheist, I assure you, by residing at Paris: yet I begin to fear that vice, or, if you will, evil, is the grand mobile of action, and that, when the passions are justly poised, we become harmless, and in the same proportion useless. (vi, pp. 444–5)

Despite the fact, however, that the gap between theoretical beliefs and practical experience is so obviously wide, and that she finds this so embittering, the letter lacks any realisation of this fact in its actual production – there is nothing in it to suggest a sense of crisis. She accepts, albeit with some chagrin, that the dregs of the past are corrupting the new, but she does not protest; rather, she submits to the intolerable by merely stating it as a fact, and even continues to assert, in the face of all the evidence: 'I cannot yet give up the hope, that a fairer day is dawning on Europe', and 'I can look beyond the evils of the moment' (vi, p. 445).

It is scarcely surprising that this letter remained unpublished. It indicates a failure of philosophical optimism – or a triumph of experience over theory – so important that it can hardly be overestimated; if it had continued, it would have required a complete reappraisal of all her most fundamental beliefs. Such a reappraisal was already being forced on many of her contemporaries, and would continue to be so over the next few years. At this time, however, Wollstonecraft was unable fully to accept the consequences, as the contradictions inherent in her next work, the *Historical and Moral View*, demonstrate.

It was about four months before she apparently felt able to start writing again. Her first extant reference to the *Historical and Moral View* can be found in a letter to her sister Eliza Bishop dated 13 June 1793, in which she says she is 'writing a great book' (Wardle (1979) p. 231). One of the most remarkable things about this book, it could be said, is the circumstances in which it was written. In Paris, the Terror – one of history's most sensational events – was being enacted; while three miles away, on the other side of Porte Maillot at Neuilly-sur-Seine, Wollstonecraft was living out a personal idyll of romantic love with Gilbert Imlay. Insulated from the outside world though she was, she could scarcely have been unaware that her friends and acquaintances were being imprisoned and executed one by one. Tom Paine, Helen Maria Williams and John Hurford Stone were among the English arrested at this time, and many of the leaders of the Girondists – including Jean-Pierre Brissot, a friend of Imlay's, and Marie Roland, who is thought to have befriended Wollstonecraft on her first arrival in Paris – were guillotined in October 1793. Indeed, Godwin wrote later that she:

> described to me, more than once, the anguish she felt at hearing of the death of Brissot, Vernigaud, and the twenty deputies, as one of the most intolerable sensations she had ever experienced. (Holmes (1987) p. 244)

Presumably her decision to start her first volume with an analysis of the beginnings of the Revolution was an attempt to explain these disturbing events to her own satisfaction. But there is no doubt that in making that choice, rather than giving a first-hand account of the events which she could have witnessed for herself in Paris, she lost the opportunity of a lifetime.

Composition of the *Historical and Moral View* seems to have proceeded slowly – interrupted, no doubt, by the pleasures as well as the complications of her relationship with Imlay, by her pregnancy and her move to Le Havre. By the following February, she was writing to Ruth Barlow that she was 'preparing part of my MS to send [to England]' (Wardle (1979) p. 249), but the work was obviously incomplete, since in the same letter she requested copies of the French Assembly's *Journal des Débats et des Décrets*, which formed part of her source material (Wardle (1979) p. 250). She had sent off the 'great part of my MS' by 10 March (*ibid.*), and the book finally appeared in September 1794, fifteen months after its inception.

As one of Wollstonecraft's reviewers (in *The British Critic* vol. vi, 1795) was quick to point out, the historical material in the *Historical and Moral View* was drawn from several sources. The reviewer demonstrated a number of borrowings from *The New Annual Register's British and Foreign History; for the Year 1791*, and also noted in passing Wollstonecraft's use of the writings of Mirabeau. In fact Wollstonecraft also made use of Rabaut's *Précis Historique*, Lally-Tollendal's *Mémoire* (1790), her friend Thomas Christie's *Letters on the Revolution in France*, and various other journals and parliamentary archives. Despite the reviewer's view of this as unacceptable practice, Wollstonecraft's purpose was less to give an account of the events – which would have been available elsewhere – than to show them in a particular light, from a clear angle of vision, as her title indicates. Indeed, the book is so heavily weighted by commentary that at the end of the first (and, in the event, only) volume of over five hundred pages, the historical account, which has reached May 1787 by Book I Chapter 3, ends in October 1789, three months after the beginning of the Revolution.

It is interesting to note a fact of which Wollstonecraft was almost certainly unaware: Godwin had been responsible for writing the historical section of the *New Annual Register* since 1784. His brief had been to write with 'no extravagances of style and only the lightest comment or judgement' (St Clair (1989) pp. 31–2), a method diametrically opposed to Wollstonecraft's own. She has little idea of history as an objective art, and does not appear to distinguish between fact, rumour and gossip, especially when she is writing about the court and the *ancien régime*. She accepts the views of those who insisted that the court was depraved, morally corrupt, incompetent and despotic, and does not attempt to distinguish between different kinds of depravity. Her historical procedures are unmethodical, to say the least, and she tends to see historical process in terms of personalities, and of cause and effect. She has already decided how wicked the *ancien régime* was before she starts, and even in passages where she is ostensibly giving a historical account of events, she inserts her own bias. Her methods may be seen in a comparison between her version of an event and the original account given in the *New Annual Register*:

> The Assembly was opened by a speech from the throne, in which the monarch declared his satisfaction at seeing himself surrounded, after

so long an interval, by the representatives of his people – he mentioned
the heavy debt of the public, a part of which had accumulated during
his own reign, but in an honourable cause . . . (*New Annual Register*
(1791) p. 6)

The states general was opened, the 5th of May, 1789, by a speech from
the throne, to which the courtiers, in the usual phraseology, would
naturally tack the epithet – *gracious*. The king commenced with a
heartless declaration of his satisfaction at seeing himself surrounded by
the representatives of his people; and then, enumerating the heavy
debts of the nation, a great part of which had accumulated during his
reign, he added one of those idle falsehoods, which swelled his
declamation without throwing dust in any one's eyes, *that it was an
honourable cause*, when it was notorious, that the cause ought to have
been reckoned most dishonourable . . . (vi, p. 56)

What is of interest to the twentieth-century reader of the *Historical
and Moral View* is not, however, the historical material, which is
widely – and presumably more reliably – available elsewhere, but
Wollstonecraft's additions to it. Recent commentators have found
little to say about the work, but it was greeted with enthusiasm by
most of its early reviewers, with the notable exception of the *British
Critic*. In addition to pointing out Wollstonecraft's borrowings, this
reviewer also took exception to her morality, disapproved of her
politics, and accused her of 'tinsel and tawdriness of style' (p. 36).
Moreover, he also found a fundamental flaw in her arguments:

Sometimes she reasons solely on what she calls first principles; at other
times her sentiments are exclusively formed on what has passed under
her observation; and the deductions from these two sources refuse all
blending, or union with each other. (vi, p. 35)

That problem, indeed, lies at the heart of the work. Far from
detracting from the book's interest, however, this in fact increases
it. Despite Godwin's assertion that the *Historical and Moral View*
was written 'with more sobriety and cheerfulness' than her earlier
'Letter Introductory' (Holmes (1987) p. 106), it is clear that many
doubts still remained in her mind about the final outcome of
events.

In her earlier writings on the Revolution Wollstonecraft had been
cautious in her expressions of millenarian enthusiasm about the
outcome of events in France, especially in comparison with some of

her contemporaries. Joseph Priestley, for example, saw the Revolution as the beginning of that 'reign of peace' which had been 'distinctly and repeatedly foretold in many prophecies, delivered more than two thousand years ago'; and Catherine Macaulay drew attention to:

> some passages in the Revelations [which] point to a time when the *iron* sceptre of *arbitrary* sway shall be broken; when *righteousness shall prevail* over the whole earth . . .[2]

It is clear, however, that the 'first principles' to which Wollstonecraft continually returns in the *Historical and Moral View* are more moderate and secular expressions of the millennialist belief, which was widely held at this time, that both men and political systems were naturally moving towards a state of perfection. As she expresses it in the Preface, the Revolution must be seen as the 'natural consequence of intellectual improvement, gradually proceeding to perfection in the advancement of communities from a state of barbarism to that of polished society' (vi, p. 7). She asserts:

> Reason has, at last, shown her captivating face, beaming with benevolence; and it will be impossible for the dark hand of despotism to obscure its radiance, or the lurking dagger of subordinate tyrants to reach her bosom. The image of God implanted in our nature is now rapidly expanding . . . (vi, p. 22)

It is noticeable that here, as in the 'Letter Introductory', Wollstonecraft takes refuge in personification and tired imagery when she wants to hide her loss of confidence. She says that she will be able to prove:

> that the people are essentially good, and that knowledge is rapidly advancing to that degree of perfectibility, when the proud distinctions of sophisticating fools will be eclipsed by the mild rays of philosophy . . . (vi, p. 46)

But many passages in the work make it clear that she is holding on to these beliefs only by means of a great intellectual effort in the face of the very different evidence offered by her observation and her feelings. In her Preface – written, it must be recalled, in the wake of the Terror and of the executions of her acquaintances among the Girondists – she admits this difficulty, and the necessity of guarding against 'the erroneous inferences of sensibility' when confronted by:

The rapid changes, the violent, the base, and nefarious assassinations, which have clouded the vivid prospect that began to spread a ray of joy and gladness over the gloomy horizon of oppression, [and] cannot fail to chill the sympathizing bosom, and palsy intellectual vigour. (vi, p. 6)

Her attempt to contemplate 'these stupendous events with the cool eye of observation' (*ibid.*) forces her to adopt various unconvincing strategies in order to reconcile theory with practice. One of these, naturally enough, involves proving her first premiss: that the progress of reason and knowledge is in the direction of continual improvement. Since the example of the most recent events in France threatens to prove otherwise, she turns to the evidence of the past. In Book II Chapter 4, she sets out a survey of world history which is intended to prove her point. As she begins with the pre-Christian era, she is forced to confront the fact that since:

> all the improvements which were made in arts and sciences were suddenly overturned, both in Greece and in Rome . . . superficial reasoners have been led to think that there is only a certain degree of civilization to which men are capable of attaining, without receding back to a state of barbarism, by the horrid consequences of anarchy. (vi, p. 109)

But these ancient civilisations, she goes on to argue, 'never extended beyond polishing the manners, often at the expense of the heart, or morals'; moreover, the fact that the 'atrocious vices and gigantic crimes' which were committed at that time have never been repeated since proves the progress of morality and reason (vi, pp. 111–12). She dismisses the Middle Ages as a period when 'Nothing . . . was founded on philosophical principles', and considers that although the Crusades 'freed many of the vassals', and the clergy was much improved during the Reformation, there was no substantial improvement in government (vi, p. 113). Britain, however, is excepted, since the British constitution, although it lacked a specific basis before 1688, rested on principles 'emanating from the consent, if not the sense, of the nation' (vi, p. 114). The example of Britain, she points out, enabled America to form its own constitution (vi, p. 115). In Europe, knowledge proceeded more slowly; but she recognises the advances in scientific knowledge made by Descartes and Newton as a factor in wearing away 'the ferocity of northern despotism', and she has nothing but praise for the court of Frederick the Great of Prussia as an example of the application of enlightened principles of knowledge and culture. By this means she arrives at her final point: that France is the first European state to have overthrown despotism, and thus represents the peak of progress so far (vi, pp. 116–17). She returns to the historical argument in her final chapter, where, under the heading 'The Progress of Reform', she argues that the development of the arts in France had softened the rigour of the old government, allowing the philosophers to form a confederation and to put together the Encyclopaedia, which had 'eluded the dangerous vigilance of absolute ministers' (vi, p. 225).

Wollstonecraft's view of Western history is obviously politically biased in the extreme, in the interest of proving her case that civilisation is proceeding towards inevitable perfection. Even so, it is unfortunately clear that she is less certain of her proof than at first appears. This is a result of the fact that although she feels certain that the overthrow of the despotic *ancien régime* represents an unarguable advance, the behaviour of the newly liberated French appears to disprove her arguments. She admits as much in the conclusion of the work, which it is difficult not to see as a retraction of all the arguments about perfectibility and progress which have gone before:

> Let us examine the catalogue of vices of men in a savage state, and contrast them with those of men civilized; we shall find, that a barbarian, considered as a moral being, is an angel, compared with the refined villain of artificial life. (vi, p. 235)

This inconsistency illustrates Wollstonecraft's chief difficulty in this work – the fact that, as she puts it in Book I Chapter 4:

> whilst the heart sickens over details of crimes and follies, and the understanding is appalled by the labour of unravelling a black tissue of plots, which exhibits the human character in the most revolting point of view, it is . . . difficult to bring ourselves to believe that out of this chaotic mass a fairer government is rising than has ever shed the sweets of social life on the world. (vi, p. 47)

She makes various attempts to find a rational solution to this problem. The simplest is to be found in the continuation of the passage: 'But things must have time to find their level' (vi, p. 47); or, as she puts it elsewhere, 'Things must be left to their natural course' (vi, p. 162), since 'the improvements in philosophy and morals have been extremely tardy. . . . [and] in the science of politics still more slow' (vi, p. 183). This may not appear, at first glance, to offer a sufficient explanation for the fact that both the mobs and the newly elected Assembly have committed atrocities; that 'disasters . . . have sullied the glories of the revolution' (vi, p. 105); that men have behaved like 'monsters' (vi, p. 125); and that 'public anarchy, and private discord, have been productive of . . . dreadful catastrophes and wanton outrages' (vi, p. 136). Wollstonecraft blames two factors for this outcome, both of which are related to what she sees as the precipitous speed with which events have proceeded.

First, she offers an argument which had been central to the *Rights of Woman*: if any section of society suffers under a long period of oppression, its capacity for moral development will be stunted. 'Just sentiments gain footing only in proportion as the understanding is enlarged by cultivation' (vi, p. 70), and 'when men live in continual fear, and know not what they have to apprehend, they always become cunning and pusillanimous' (vi, p. 75). Thus, the French aristocracy have only themselves to blame; the rich have:

> for ages tyrannized over the poor, teaching them how to act when possessed of power, and now they must feel the consequence. People are rendered ferocious by misery . . . (vi, p. 46)

Since she condemns 'the wild notions of original sin' (vi, p. 21), and believes (with Rousseau) that 'the human heart is naturally good' (vi, p. 54), it follows that 'when men once see . . . that on the general happiness depends their own, reason will give strength to the fluttering wings of passion . . .' (vi, p. 21). Some external stimulus is clearly needed for this realisation to take place, and freedom from oppression, however desirable, is not in itself enough. Positive social change – which in this case must originate from a restructuring of the system of government – is also required, since 'the faculties of man are unfolded and perfected by the improvements made to society' (vi, p. 20).

It might be supposed that Wollstonecraft could be justifiably optimistic about this prospect, given the fact that France had just undergone enormous and fundamental political changes. But although she sees the situation which existed in August 1789 as 'the point the most advantageous in which a government was ever constructed', and is wholly in favour of the Declaration of Rights, which she sees as evidence that 'reason was tracing out the road which leads to virtue, glory and happiness' (vi, p. 143), she views many of the decisions made by the Assembly as at best rash and at worst disastrous. Again, she blames the speed at which changes have been made:

> from the commencement of the revolution, the misery of France has originated from the folly or art of men, who have spurred the people on too fast; tearing up prejudices by the root, which they should have permitted to die away gradually. (vi, p. 159)

She deplores the execution of Louis XVI, arguing that he should have been put into the care of another European monarchy, or allowed 'a small portion of liberty and power' (vi, p. 160). While she is theoretically in favour of a republic, she argues that such a system is suitable only for a civilisation which has reached a much higher degree of perfection than that so far attained by France (vi, p. 162). She is unsympathetic to what she sees as a mistaken decision, on the part of the representatives, not to form an upper chamber, which she believes would have acted as a check on the excesses of what she has earlier called 'desperate and impudent smatterers in politics' (vi, p. 136); their fears that such a chamber would have become 'the asylum of a new aristocracy' can, she argues, 'only be accounted for by recollecting the many cruel thraldoms, from which they had so recently escaped' (vi, p. 164). Instead of taking as their model Hume's Idea of a Perfect Commonwealth, an example which their present level of development rendered unsuitable because it represented too high an ideal to be immediately practicable ('the revolution of states should be gradual'), she suggests that the French should have adopted a version of the American or the English plan. She hastens to add that this need not lead to a condemnation of the theory itself as 'absurd and chimerical' (vi, pp. 166–7); she attributes the problem to the fact that too ideal and too difficult a model was fixed on too quickly.

All Wollstonecraft's best efforts at rationalisation are threatened with defeat when her account reaches 5 October 1789, the occasion of the women's march to Versailles, which she calls 'one of the blackest of the machinations that have since the revolution disgraced the dignity of man, and sullied the annals of humanity' (vi, p. 206). This was, of course, the very same event which had so outraged Burke, whose account of it had formed the centrepiece of *Reflections*. In her reply, Wollstonecraft had defended the women of Paris against Burke's – admittedly hyperbolic – condemnation. She cannot condemn the women herself, in the *Historical and Moral View*, without, presumably, losing face as well as abandoning her feminist principles. Nevertheless, she has to confront the fact that they had acted like 'a set of monsters, distinct from the people' – a statement which indicates the degree to which she had sentimentalised the concept of 'the people'. Thus, she adopts a view which was commonly held at the time, and attributes the organisation of the march to the Duc d'Orléans, whom she finds guilty of 'the grossest libertinism, seasoned with vulgarity. . . . his heart was as tainted as the foul atmosphere he breathed' (vi, p. 207). This bias provides a fine demonstration of the extent to which she accepted popular supposition without question. Mirabeau, a favourite of the revolutionaries, of whom she wholeheartedly approves, was certainly a libertine. Orléans, who had thrown in his lot with the revolutionaries and had voted in the Assembly for the execution of his cousin Louis XVI, was an extremely accomplished man: presumably Wollstonecraft attacks him because he was not only a *débauché* but also a rich landowner and an aristocrat of the royal house. As a recent critical essay has pointed out, he has taken on the role of archetypal villain in Wollstonecraft's text, while Marie Antoinette assumes the ambivalent roles of both the 'personification of aristocratic luxury' and the innocent corrupted by patriarchy, and finally victimised and violated (Jones (1992) pp. 185–7, 197).

In fact, Orléans had nothing whatever to do with the march on Versailles. Her source for the supposition that he did may have been the account of events published by the *Annual Register for the Year 1790* (1793):

> There are the strongest reasons for supposing, that the Orléans cabal, though assisted and supported by the republicans on very different grounds, were the immediate and principal authors of the present disturbances; none other could, in any degree, equally influence and command the rabble of that city, as the faction in question. (p. 47)

The events of 5–6 October obviously affected Wollstonecraft powerfully. It is interesting to note that the strength of her reaction seems to be largely a result of what she sees as a desecration of the privacy of the king and queen, which she describes using a mixture of religious and sexual metaphors; the massacre of the guards appears to be considerably less important to her:

> The altar of humanity had been profaned – The dignity of freedom had been tarnished – The sanctuary of repose, the asylum of care and fatigue, the chaste temple of a woman, I consider the queen only as one . . . was violated in murderous fury – The life of the king was assailed, when he had acceded to all their demands – And, when their plunder was snatched from them, they massacred the guards, who were only doing their duty . . . (vi, p. 209)

It would be easy to see this account, taken out of context, as wholly conservative – it could almost have come from the pen of Burke. The fact that it comes almost at the end of the volume possibly led Janet Todd to write of the *Historical and Moral View* that 'the second half . . . is harsher than the first' (Todd (1976) p. 4). Passages throughout the book, however, clearly demonstrate that for all her assertions to the contrary, Wollstonecraft's revulsion and despair frequently threaten to overturn her optimism.

In Book II Chapter 2, for example, she presents herself as weeping over the former oppressions of France, and eager to report the fall of the Bastille; but she is at once led to the recollection that the fortress is still used for 'the victims of revenge and suspicion', and her praise takes on a very different character from that which, presumably, she had originally intended:

> Down fell the temple of despotism; but – despotism has not been buried in its ruins! – Unhappy country! – when will thy children cease to tear thy bosom? (vi, p. 85)

When she confines herself to a straighforward account of the events of 14 July, she manages for the most part to present them as 'a nation shaking off its fetters' (vi, p. 93), 'a splendid example, to prove, that nothing can resist a people determined to live free' (vi, p. 100); but the ambivalence of her attitude is made plain by the fact that these optimistic assertions are constantly undercut by indications that she is profoundly troubled. Her pleasure in the contemplation of 'the superiority of a nation rising in its own defence' is 'depressed by the recollection of the sinister events which have since clouded the bright beams' (vi, p. 103); she is unable to forget the 'disasters [which] have sullied the glories of the revolution' and brought on 'the most fatal calamities' (vi, p. 105); and although, she says, 'lively, sanguine minds' rejoiced when freedom rose up 'like a lion rouzed from his lair', the result has been the deplorable fact that 'the dogs of war have been let loose, and corruption has swarmed with noxious life' (vi, p. 106). When she returns to the fall of the Bastille, in Book III Chapter 1, her support for violent change appears to have been eroded to such an extent that she now finds herself arguing that it might have been better if the fortress had not fallen at all:

> It is true, had the national assembly been allowed quietly to have made some reforms . . . the Bastille, though tottering on its dungeons, might yet have stood erect. – And if it had, the sum of human misery could scarcely have been increased. For the *guillotine* not finding it's [*sic*] way to the splendid square it had polluted, streams of innocent blood would not have flowed . . . (vi, p. 123)

It is interesting to note that Godwin makes particular mention of how disturbed Wollstonecraft had been by a first-hand experience of the effects of the guillotine:

> she happened one day to enter Paris by foot . . . when an execution, attended with some peculiar aggravations, had just taken place, and the blood of the guillotine appeared fresh on the pavement. The emotions of her soul burst forth in indignant exclamations . . . (Holmes (1987) p. 244)

Again, in Book V Chapter 3, she follows a passage in praise of the beauties of Paris (which should be compared with the impression given of the city in her 'Letter Introductory', where she sees no beauty, no 'proportion and harmony' in the buildings) with the reflection that 'this prospect of delights' quickly vanishes when one sees:

> The cavalcade of death [moving] along, shedding mildew over all the beauties of the scene, and blasting every joy! The elegance of the palaces is revolting, when they are viewed as prisons, and the sprightliness of the people disgusting, when they are hastening to view the operations of the guillotine, or carelessly passing over the earth stained with blood. (vi, p. 216)

Then, with 'bitterness of soul', the city is seen as 'a nest of crimes' – not, of course, the crimes of the *ancien régime*, but those of the present government. Other examples of the same kind can be found throughout the book. Indeed, if the work is read carefully, it becomes difficult to see why many twentieth-century commentators have described Wollstonecraft's attitude as optimistic.[3]

Although Wollstonecraft's account reaches only as far as 19 October 1789, her perspective is inevitably coloured by the fact that she was writing in 1793, with all the added wisdom of hindsight. Certainly a comparison with the reaction of other expatriate observers at this period suggests that until at least 1792 it was possible to view in a remarkably optimistic light occurrences which would later seem to point forward to the excesses of Robespierre and the Reign of Terror. The British travel writer Arthur Young, for example, who had written in his *Travels During the Years 1787, 1788 and 1789* (1792) that 'the extent and universality of oppression under which the people groaned' was such that 'a revolution was . . . absolutely necessary to the welfare of the kingdom' (pp. 539–40), was so shocked by the events of 1792 and early 1793 that he took the opposite view in his next work, *The Example of France a Warning to Britain* (1793):

> [The Revolution] has brought more misery, poverty, devastation, imprisonment, bloodshed, and ruin on France, in four years, than the old government did in a century . . . [it] has absolutely ruined the kingdom . . . the old government of France, with all its faults, was certainly the best enjoyed by any considerably [*sic*] country in Europe. (pp. 13–14, 35, 36)

Helen Maria Williams, who had lived in France since July 1790, had strenuously asserted in the first volume of her *Letters Written in France* (1790) that the rumours reaching England of 'crimes, assassinations, torture and death' were greatly exaggerated, and that although reflections on the bloodshed gave rise to 'gloomy images', she felt that gains had been made at 'a far cheaper rate than could have been expected' (Williams (1790) pp. 16–17, 81–2). However, by 1793 she too was forced to speak of 'anarchy', of 'sanguinary rites', of 'infernal executions', and of the 'deep and extraordinary malignity' of Robespierre, although she continued to assert that '*the foundation was laid in wisdom*' (Williams (1793) iii, p. 17, iv, p. 269).

Another account was given by William Wordsworth, who – as a convinced anti-monarchist – had arrived in Paris on 29 October 1792 on his way back to England from Orléans. He describes his mood at the time as one in which 'enflamed with hope', he viewed the crimes perpetrated in the name of the Revolution as 'Ephemeral monsters, to be seen but once,/Things that could only shew themselves and die'

(Wordsworth (1985) p. 360). Nevertheless, his account of the unexpected turmoil of mind which he experienced during his first night
in Paris is remarkably similar to the imaginative confusion described
a few months later in Wollstonecraft's December letter to Johnson:

> I thought of those September massacres,
> Divided from me by a little month,
> And felt and touched them, a substantial dread . . .
> 'The horse is taught his manage, and the wind
> Of heaven wheels round and treads in his own steps;
> Year follows year, the tide returns again,
> Day follows day, all things have second birth;
> The earthquake is not satisfied at once' –
> And in such way I wrought upon myself,
> Until I seemed to hear a voice that cried
> To the whole city, 'Sleep no more!'
> (Wordsworth (1985) pp. 360, 362)

Wordsworth's doubts and fears over the course of the next two years
– the deep divisions created in his mind by France's declaration of
war on England, the 'melancholy' days and disturbed nights which
he experienced during the Reign of Terror, his exultation at hearing
of the death of Robespierre, and his subsequent disappointment when
the 'golden times' for which he hoped failed to materialise – are all
described in detail in *The Prelude*. He concludes this account by
describing how, much in need of a new source of philosophical
optimism, he turned to Godwin's *Political Justice*, since, he says, he
still 'had hope to see/ . . . The man to come parted as by a gulph/From
him who had been' (Wordsworth (1985) p. 418) – a hope which was
vitally relevant at a time when the man 'who had been' – in
revolutionary France, at least – had shown himself capable of
inconceivable atrocities. Thus, as Hazlitt wrote, 'No work in our time
gave such a blow to the philosophical mind of the country as the
celebrated *Enquiry Concerning Political Justice*'. (Hazlitt (1930–34) xi,
p. 17). Clearly, this effect was attributable largely to Godwin's cer-
tainties about man's ultimate perfectibility. His confident assertion
that: 'It requires no great degree of fortitude to look with indifference
on the false fire of the moment and to foresee the calm period of reason
which will succeed' (Godwin (1793) i, p. xii) offered a tempting
antidote to the intellectual confusion which was, increasingly,
assailing supporters of revolutionary principles.

It is noticeable, of course, that Wollstonecraft's attempts to counteract her own growing confusion and despair rest mainly on assertions of the ultimate perfectibility of mankind and of political systems, which receives greater emphasis in this work than in any of her previous writings. The publication of Godwin's *Political Justice*, in February 1793, coincided with Wollstonecraft's deep depression and loss of faith, demonstrated in her 'Letter Introductory' (composed the same month). Since she was undoubtedly kept supplied with books and literary magazines by her friends in England, it seems highly likely that she read Godwin's book during the spring or early summer of 1793, and that its optimistic philosophy enabled her to attempt the more positive view of events upon which she embarked in June of that year. Although this is impossible to prove, there are certainly passages in the *Historical and Moral View* which appear to be resoundingly Godwinian, such as the assertion that:

> Reason has at last shown her captivating face, beaming with benevolence; and it will be impossible for the dark hand of despotism again to obscure its radiance, or the lurking dagger of tyrants to reach her bosom. (vi, p. 19)

It is possible, however, that the similarities of terminology could be attributed to a common source in the literature of rational dissent, to which both Godwin and Wollstonecraft owed much of their thinking.[4]

At all events, whatever the stimulus was for Wollstonecraft's attempt to present an optimistic and positive view of the events in France, it proved to be only fitfully and temporarily effective. Her declared intention, in the Preface, of exercising 'the cool eye of observation' (vi, p. vii), led – as the *British Critic* astutely pointed out – to conclusions which frequently acted in complete opposition to her declared 'first principles'.

Chapter 6

◆

Letters Written During a Short Residence in Sweden, Norway and Denmark (1796)

Wollstonecraft returned to London in April 1795 to find that Imlay was involved with another woman, and was no longer willing to live with her. Throughout the following months she lived apart from him, and began to ask the question that dominates the rest of her correspondence with him: 'whether you desire to live with me, or part forever?'.[1] 'Grief has a firm hold on my heart', she wrote on 27 May (vi, p. 406); and in early June, according to Godwin's *Memoirs*, she attempted suicide (Holmes (1987) p. 249).[2] A week or so later, she set out on 'this new expedition' to Scandinavia on Imlay's behalf (*ibid.*). Although it clearly must have been convenient for Imlay to find something to occupy her as well as to keep her at a distance, the venture was an important and serious one, the details of which have emerged only comparatively recently.

Briefly, Imlay had been involved in the purchase and fitting out of a ship, the *Maria and Margaretha*, which, although registered as a Norwegian cargo ship, was in fact carrying silver and plate valued at £3,500 – presumably the property of dispossessed aristocrats – out of France to Gothenburg in Sweden. This was a highly risky and illegal enterprise, as it involved breaking the British blockade which was in force to prevent trade between France and Scandinavia. The ship failed to arrive, and initially Imlay was informed that it had sunk. It later transpired, however, that the captain, Peder Ellefsen, had returned to his home at Risør in Norway, having apparently appropriated the treasure for his own use. The Danish Royal

Commission undertook to investigate the disappearance, but Imlay clearly felt that personal enquiries should also be made, and this was the extraordinarily delicate and difficult task with which Wollstonecraft was entrusted.[3] The whole journey took almost four months. She arrived in Hull on 10 June, although as her ship was delayed until the 21st she did not arrive in Gothenburg until 27 June. Her account of her travels through Sweden into Norway, back through Sweden and Denmark to Hamburg, ending with her arrival in Dover on 4 October, in the form of letters to her 'friend' Imlay, was published in January 1796 as *Letters Written During a Short Residence in Sweden, Norway and Denmark*.[4]

Travel literature was a popular genre in the eighteenth century, and one about which Wollstonecraft had clear and definite opinions. Travel writers should, she believed, have 'some decided point of view, a grand object of pursuit to concentrate their thoughts and connect their reflections' (*Analytical Review*, 5 (1798): vii, p. 161). 'The art of travelling', she wrote in another review, 'is only a branch of the art of thinking' (vii, p. 277). In fact, to call Wollstonecraft's *Letters from Sweden* a travel book is at once accurate and diminishing. When Godwin wrote that 'perhaps a book of travels that so irresistibly seizes on the heart, never, in any other instance, found its way from the press' (Holmes (1987) p. 249), he was demonstrating a response – which has been shared by many subsequent readers – to the fact that in this book Wollstonecraft reveals more of herself, of her emotions, than in any of her earlier works.

In combining observation, reflection and autobiography, Wollstonecraft could be said in some respects to have been following popular writers such as Smollett (*Travels through France and Italy* (1766)) and Sterne (*A Sentimental Journey through France and Italy* (1768)), a work to which Wollstonecraft refers in *Letters from Sweden* (vi, p. 280). Although the *Letters from Sweden* is closer in spirit to the sensibility of Sterne than to the irascibility of Smollett, it also owes much to the writings of Rousseau. In its combination of personal confession and intense appreciation of the natural world, it perhaps most closely resembles his posthumously published autobiographical works, *Les Confessions* (1781–2) and *Les Rêveries du promeneur solitaire* (1782). Indeed, even the form of the *Letters from Sweden* seems to owe something to that of the *Promeneur solitaire*, in which each walk encompasses one of a series of reflective and self-analytical meditations. Wollstonecraft was later to refer to herself as a *Solitary Walker* (Wardle (1979) p. 337).

Many models could be suggested for the rhapsodic passages in which Wollstonecraft describes her response to the beauty and sublimity of the natural world. In Rousseau's *Julie; ou La nouvelle Héloïse* (1761), for example, the hero turns to nature to soothe the anguish of his thwarted love. Wollstonecraft – or the heroine of the *Letters from Sweden* – shared the betrayal, the sense of total rejection, experienced by the hero of Goethe's *Die Leiden des Jungen Werthers* (1774), as well as his rhapsodic response to nature. Wollstonecraft would also certainly have read Marie Roland's *Voyage en Suisse* (1787), in which Roland had written:

> On n'oublie pas, mais on ne sauroit décrire, ce lieu spirituel et romantique, où l'áme s'élève à l'unisson de la nature, où les grandes scènes ravissent l'imagination, ramènent aux sentiments profonds, à la méditation d'objets sublimes, à l'enthousiasme qui rend meilleur et plus heureux . . .[5]

Even though it is possible to point to these various literary ancestors, it must be said that Wollstonecraft's work is breaking new ground in every sense. Her itinerary, for one thing, was an uncommon one: most travellers visited only France, Spain, Italy and Holland. The *New Cambridge Bibliography of English Literature* lists, among scores of travel books written during the second half of the eighteenth century, only seven which deal even in passing with the Scandinavian countries – in *Letters from Sweden* Wollstonecraft refers ironically to one of these, William Coxe's *Travels into Poland, Russia, Sweden and Denmark* (1790) ('as for the hills, "capped with *eternal* snow", Mr Coxe's description led me to look for them; but they had flown' (vi, p. 304)). Another difference between *Letters from Sweden* and other contemporary travel books is the highly politicised nature of Wollstonecraft's commentary: although she has modified some of her views about France and the Revolution, she still sees the Scandinavian countries as societies which are in grave need of the kind of 'improvement' which, at least in her more optimistic moments, she continues to view as inevitable. But it is the autobiographical content of the *Letters from Sweden* which makes the work unique: the fact that Wollstonecraft was a woman, travelling without a husband but accompanied for part of the journey by her small child and a nursemaid, on an obviously specific but unstated errand which took her into the wilds of Scandinavia; and, moreover, the fact that her letters frequently refer to a deeply unhappy emotional situation in which she is involved with their (unnamed) recipient. Thus, as in all her mature works, Wollstonecraft is making use of a popular genre while simultaneously subverting it.

According to her Advertisement, Wollstonecraft's plan was 'simply to endeavour to give a just view of the present state of the countries I have passed through' (vi, p. 241); accordingly, the greatest part of the *Letters from Sweden* consists of her observations on the political, social and domestic customs prevalent in the countries she travels through, and of geographical descriptions. But as she says at the beginning of the work, the fact that she chose to write in the form of letters meant that she 'could not avoid being continually the first person – "the little hero of each tale"'; indeed, she makes it clear that the informality of the style and the personal nature of the content are intentional, challenging the reader to 'shut the book' if they have no wish to get to know her better (vi, p. 241).

The 'public' correspondence with Imlay which is represented by the *Letters from Sweden* should be read in conjunction with Wollstonecraft's personal letters to him as she waited for the favourable wind which would allow her to embark from Hull to Scandinavia, and during the voyage itself, which clearly indicate her state of mind. She certainly expects her exertions on his behalf to draw them closer together, as her letter to him from Hull on 12 June indicates (vi, p. 410). But she also wishes him to know how her health has been injured by her 'grief' at his treatment of her: 'I am not quite well'; 'I wake in the morning in violent fits of trembling' (14 June: vi, p. 410). She feels that she is 'fading away – perishing beneath a cruel blight' (16 June: vi, p. 412). She suffers from 'a violent headache', and has 'the most terrifying dreams, in which I often meet you with different casts of countenance' (18 June: vi, p. 413). Shortly after her arrival in Gothenburg, she describes falling 'senseless on the rocks. . . . I was in a stupour for a quarter of an hour' (27 June: vi, p. 416). During the early part of the journey she makes some attempts at optimism, and writes several times that her health, and her appearance, are beginning to improve: 'The rosy fingers of health already streak my cheeks – and I have seen a *physical* life in my eyes' (4 July: vi, p. 419). But these assertions – partly motivated, no doubt, by a desire to appear more like her own earlier and, to Imlay, more attractive self – are juxtaposed with indications that she constantly thinks of death, or of throwing herself off the rocks. She sees the peace of death as a welcome alternative to the torments of life without Imlay. She also sees her death as a punishment for him. Knowing in her heart that he wishes to be rid of her, she none the less believes that if she killed herself her death would harm him, afflicting him with regret, repentance and remorse. Indeed, it was in this frame of mind that she did attempt suicide shortly after her return from Scandinavia.

The personal letters are a faithful record of the psychopathology of despair following her rejection. They were certain – indeed, could not have been better designed – to alienate further the affections of someone such as Imlay. Their raw honesty leads her into contradictions, pleadings, bullyings, blackmail and constant repetition of her demand that they live together or part for ever, with her clear refusal to accept the latter alternative. She could not really believe that her value to him was not at least such that he would not be able to contemplate complete separation from her. She seriously overestimated him, because she herself could not admit such a separation. There is little doubt that so far as he was concerned, her letters confirmed what he wanted to think – that she was disturbed; that she wished to own him, to restrict his free spirit; that she was a burden, a domineering, nagging woman who made his life impossible. He was, it is certain, blind to her qualities as a person. It is ironic that, having written that men were tyrants and marriage was mere prostitution, she chose a man who went a long way to fulfilling those prophecies by becoming the father of her child in a kind of marriage.

The question of whether Wollstonecraft intended to write a travel book when she left for Scandinavia, or whether she simply adapted letters which she had already written to Imlay, has occupied her biographers. Charles Kegan Paul maintained that the *Letters from Sweden* formed part of her regular correspondence with Gilbert Imlay, and this suggestion has been taken up more recently by Claire Tomalin. Ralph Wardle, on the other hand, thinks it 'highly improbable . . . that [she] would have put Imlay to the expense of postage of the twenty-five bulky letters which make up the volume', and suggests that it may have been a journal intended for Imlay's eyes – a suggestion which has been accepted by Richard Holmes in his recent edition of the *Letters from Sweden*.[6]

If the letters were not sent, then the form of *Letters from Sweden* is fictive, and questions legitimate to ask of other fictions must apply. But lovers characteristically talk mentally, and continuously, with those they love. This is particularly true when they experience things they wish to share with their absent lovers. There can be no doubt whatsoever of Wollstonecraft's wish to share her experiences with Imlay. In view of this, the authenticity of the letters as letters becomes ambiguous and possibly irrelevant. None the less, she remains the heroine of her own fiction; he is for all time the villain. The relationship between heroine and villain colours all else in this fiction: the action is largely temporal and geographic – travelling through time and space – but the plot, the conflict, resides in the clash between protagonist and narrator in alliance on the one side, and antagonist on the other. The work moves towards disappointment (he does not meet her at Basle) and disillusion (she ceases to believe he ever intended to), though her movement homeward is not marked by an increasing sense of reality, only by a returning sense of hope and a renewal of the bitterness of another rejection.

The fiction defines the isolation and despair of the heroine, a tortured spirit betrayed by the warmth and generosity of her womanhood, by a man who exploits her, tyrannises over her, and rejects her when he has no further use for her. As an unmarried mother she has nothing but the ostracism of society to look forward to. She becomes a representative Woman, and writes a more moral tale than she ever knew: a fiction that might well have been written as a warning to women, the story of what happens when women sin and find, too late, that men betray. Had it been presented as fiction, we would have to compliment the author on her extraordinary ability to articulate the distress of her heroine – her inner suffering, often unbalancing her mind; her courage in continuing to struggle against what increasingly appear to the reader to be overwhelming circumstances; her attachment to her child; her belief in God, whom she finds in the beauties of nature and who, though he brings immediate comfort, does not bring any lasting sense of peace or fulfilment. She has, of course, no sense of sin, at least in the sense of regret or remorse for her own 'wickedness'. Indeed, she tends to embrace rather than reject the sensuality that brought her to this pass.

The fiction is marked by the strength of the narrator's feelings. Her continuing eroticism is most evident in her sense of sensual frustration: her feelings and her mind are often at odds with each other. Her determination to be independent is constantly undermined by her recognition of a powerful need for Imlay which makes her dependent on him for her well-being. As a work of fiction *Letters from*

Sweden needs to be supplemented by the personal letters to Imlay written at the same time, although for the most part these only underline and make more explicit what is undoubtedly there. Wollstonecraft's rejection and betrayal, so movingly articulated, become an archetype of man's unfeeling despotism and woman's sense of the injustice of the arrangements between the sexes. But even the Victorians could not have objected to the moral which the work generates: sin leads to grief, to despair; sin without remorse, without repentance, leads to further sin, the wages of which is death.

Wollstonecraft marries her 'novel' to her travel book – the journey through the wilderness is more real than allegorical, but it can also be read as allegorical. A good deal of her attention is directed inwards; a large part of the book consists of reflections and introspection, the result of a mind travelling in a world of its own creation.[7] The landscapes of Scandinavia also become landscapes of mind, of silence, of elevation of soul, of aesthetic satisfactions or emotional frustrations. As she says in her Apology at the end of the book:

> Private business and cares have frequently so absorbed me, as to prevent my obtaining all the information, during this journey, which the novelty of the scenes would have afforded, had my attention been continally awake to enquiry. This insensibility to present objects I have often had occasion to lament . . . (vi, p. 346)

The work is self-absorbed – to the point, perhaps, where we cannot doubt that the narrator, her mind, feelings, conflicts and obsessions, are the real subjects, the actual scenery surveyed and travelled through. In some ways she could be said to have found the objective correlative poets are said to seek, as a means of embodying their thoughts and feelings in the poems. Certainly in *Letters from Sweden* she produced a more convincing psychological fiction than she achieved in her novels.

Although the autobiographical nature of the book is undoubtedly what has attracted readers to it, the less obviously personal material is also of interest. Wollstonecraft's own opinions are seldom, if ever, absent from her observations about the social and political conditions of the Scandinavian countries; indeed, her emotional state and her feelings about Imlay colour many of her judgements. A theme which emerges in the *Letters from Sweden*, for example, is that of the corrupting influence of commerce. Wollstonecraft's journey was undertaken as a direct result of the failure of one of Imlay's financial speculations, and it could be said that she is participating in the very enterprise she condemns. But the intricacies of her relationship to Imlay, and her need to find excuses for his changed behaviour towards her, lead her to take a rather puritanical attitude: 'What is speculation, but a species of gambling, I might have said fraud' (vi, p. 304). Towards the end of the work (as her frail belief in Imlay's reawakened interest in her decreases) she speaks with increasing harshness of 'the baneful effect of extensive speculations on the moral character' (vi, p. 342), although she is willing to admit that her adverse reaction is the result of personal bias:

> men entirely devoted to commerce never acquire, or lose, all taste and greatness of mind. An ostentatious display of wealth without elegance, and a greedy enjoyment of pleasure without sentiment, embrutes. . . . But you will say that I am growing bitter, perhaps, personal. Ah! shall I whisper to you – that you – yourself, are – strangely altered, since you have entered deeply into commerce . . . (vi, p. 340)

The autobiographical material also modifies the feminism of the *Letters from Sweden*. The fact that the narrator is a woman travelling on business without a male escort demonstrates the fact that – as Wollstonecraft had pointed out in the *Rights of Woman* – women can engage in work normally undertaken by men. She never alludes overtly to this fact, although she does ensure that her readers are kept aware of the unusual nature of her position: in Letter One, for example, she says of her arrival at a lonely cottage:

> I was not sorry to see a female figure, though I had not, like Marguerite, been thinking of robberies, murder, or that other evil which instantly, as the sailors would have said, runs foul of a woman's imagination. (vi, p. 245)

Later in the same letter she relays a comment made by her host, who 'told me bluntly that I was a woman of observation, for I asked him *men's questions*' (vi, p. 248) – the understated irony of her emphasis is attractively unmistakeable.

Explicit feminist arguments are not entirely absent from the book, and again they are almost invariably connected with her own feelings and experiences. She notes, for example, that in Sweden the most menial and unpleasant tasks, such as washing the linen in an ice-cold river, are left to the women: 'Still the men stand up for the dignity of man, by oppressing the women' (vi, p. 253); in Denmark she writes:

I have every where been struck by one characteristic difference in the conduct of the two sexes; women, in general, are seduced by their superiors, and men jilted by their inferiors; rank and manners awe the one, and cunning and wantonness subjugate the other; ambition creeping into the woman's passion, and tyranny giving force to the man's; for most men treat their mistresses as kings do their favourites; *ergo* is not man then the tyrant of creation?

Still harping on the same subject, you will exclaim – How can I avoid it, when most of the struggles of an eventful life have been occasioned by the oppressed state of my sex: we reason deeply, when we forcibly feel. (vi, p. 325)

On a more personal note, in Letter Six, as she travels alone into Norway, she reflects on her feelings about leaving sixteen-month-old Fanny for the first time. The optimism which characterises the feminism of the *Rights of Woman* is not much in evidence in this passage, which seems almost like a reversion to the gloomy perspective of *Mary* in its suggestion that a woman is defeated both by too much feminine feeling ('sensibility', 'delicacy of sentiment') and by the (masculine?) development of her intellect:

You know that as a female I am particularly attached to her – I feel more than a mother's fondness when I reflect on the oppressed state of her sex. I dread lest she should be forced to sacrifice her heart to her principles, or her principles to her heart. With trembling hand I shall cultivate sensibility, or cherish delicacy of sentiment, lest, while I lend fresh blushes to the rose, I sharpen the thorns that will wound the breast I would fain guard – I dread to unfold her mind, lest it should render her unfit for the world she is to inhabit – Hapless woman! what a fate is thine! (vi, p. 269)

The deliberate irony of Wollstonecraft's use of the conventional imagery of thorns and roses for seduction, submission and betrayal is inevitably coloured by the bitterness of her own personal experience. Although her concern is for the education and fate of her own child, there is perhaps some indication here, and elsewhere in the work, of a modification to Wollstonecraft's attitude to women – in *Letters from Sweden* she tends to assume a representative role as far as her sex is concerned, and her fate becomes the fate of womankind, whereas it has been suggested that in the *Rights of Woman* she shows a lack of fellow feeling for other women (Lorch (1990) p. 89). Her social and historical accounts in *Letters from Sweden* are often constructed around female oppression by a patriarchal society. She tells in Letter Eight, for example, how her compassion has been aroused by the discovery that a young girl who is acting as wet nurse to the landlady of an inn where she is staying is paid twelve dollars a year, of which ten goes to the nurse for her own child, and that her husband has 'run away to get clear of the expence' (vi, p. 283). In Letter Thirteen she expresses her sympathy for the 'unfortunate Matilda', sister to George III, who had been married to the mentally retarded King Christian VII of Denmark, and had died at the age of 24 after a tragic love affair with the court physician, Johann Frederick Struensee (vi, p. 321–2).

It is also noticeable that, although she is still sometimes troubled by the 'total want of chastity' among the lower classes (vi, p. 258), the puritanism which characterised parts of the *Rights of Woman* is nowhere to be found, and – presumably as a result of her own experience of sexuality – her tolerance seems to have increased, most notably when she writes approvingly of the period which she calls 'a kind of interregnum between the reign of the father and the husband', which is:

> the only period of freedom and pleasure that the women enjoy. Young people, who are attached to each other . . . exchange rings, and are permitted to enjoy a degree of liberty which I have never noticed in any other country. The days of courtship are therefore prolonged, till it be perfectly convenient to marry: the intimacy often becomes very tender: and if the lover obtain the privilege of a husband, it can only be termed half by stealth, because the family is wilfully blind. (vi, p. 326)

Many of Wollstonecraft's most fundamental ideas and theories had been called into question during her stay in Paris, and her honesty had been such that she was forced to admit their possible fallibility even at the expense of overturning her primary argument. In the *Letters from Sweden* it is possible to see the process of change continuing – altered attitudes towards women and towards sexuality are just two examples – although she does continue to adhere to some of the principles she has carried with her from the beginning. But although she appears to have revised some of her ideas about France and about the Revolution, it is clear that she has not abandoned her political radicalism. In *Letters from Sweden*, as elsewhere in her writings, her political views are frequently expressed in terms which sail dangerously close to the wind of political cliché – 'Despotism, as is usually the case, I found had here [Sweden] cramped the industry of man' (vi, p. 243); 'Here [Christiania] I saw the cloven foot of despotism' (vi, p. 305); 'under whatever point of view I consider society, it appears, to me, that an adoration of property is the root of all evil' (vi, p. 325). Ideas about man's perfectibility, which had been severely tested in Paris, emerge from time to time in *Letters from Sweden* – mainly, it seems, as a ploy to bolster her flagging optimism in less than ideal circumstances. In Letter Ten, for example, she writes that on her arrival in Laurvig, finding herself in the midst of a group of lawyers, her 'head turned round, [her] heart grew sick, as [she] regarded visages deformed by vice'; but she comforts herself with the idea that '[t]hese locusts will probably diminish, as the people become more enlightened' (vi, p. 290). In the next letter (written from Risør) she reflects on the lack of delicacy and taste among the female inhabitants, but remarks: 'I could perceive even here the first steps of the improvement which I am persuaded will make a very obvious progress in the course of half a century. . . . Improving manners will lead to finer moral feelings' (vi, p. 297). Earlier in the same letter, however, her speculations have taken a more pessimistic turn. As she sailed along the wild Norwegian coast, she writes:

> I anticipated the future improvement of the world, and observed how much man had still to do, to obtain of the earth all it could yield. I even carried my speculations so far as to advance a million or two years to the moment when the earth would perhaps be so perfectly cultivated, and so completely peopled, as to render it necessary to inhabit every spot. Imagination went still farther, and pictured the state of man when the earth could no longer support him. Where was he to fly to from universal famine? Do not smile: I really became distressed for these fellow creatures, yet unborn. (vi, pp. 294–5)

Although she remains a radical, and at least a part-time believer in human perfectibility, Wollstonecraft's experiences in Scandinavia do have the effect of modifying her retrospections on France, on the character of the French, and on the Revolution in general. As early as Letter One she finds herself making a comparison between the 'sluggish inhabitants' of Sweden and the Parisians, whose taste for novelty and curiosity she asserts to be 'a proof of the progress they had made in refinement' (vi, p. 245) – a complete reversal of the attitudes she had expressed in the 'Letter Introductory' and the *Historical and Moral View*. Later in the work she admits openly that she is revising her ideas: 'I believe I should have been less severe in the remarks I have made on the vanity and depravity of the french, had I travelled towards the north before I visited France' (vi, p. 326). This is a result of her general disappointment with what she has managed to observe of the national character of the Scandinavians. She has seen little to confirm the popular belief about the 'virtues of a rising people'; on the contrary, she has come to appreciate the 'virtuous enthusiasm' shown by the common people of France, which, she believes, goes a long way to balance 'the account of horrours' (*ibid.*). In any case, writing *Letters from Sweden* outside France and after the death of Robespierre, she is able to assert that 'Robespierre was a monster', and seems to suggest that she lays the blame for the atrocities in France at his door (vi, p. 302). It does appear, indeed, that her faith in revolutionary principles never entirely recovered from the first shock of despair which her 'Letter Introductory' demonstrates. This, at least, seems to be the message of the final paragraph of the *Letters from Sweden*:

> An ardent affection for the human race makes enthusiastic characters eager to produce alteration in laws and governments prematurely. To render them useful and permanent, they must be the growth of each particular soil, and the gradual fruit of the ripening understanding of the nation, matured by time, not forced by an unnatural fermentation. (vi, p. 346)

In many ways the logical outcome of her insistence, in the *Historical and Moral View*, that change must take place slowly, this passage nevertheless suggests that her thinking had moved on by this time to the point where she was able to admit – as she had been unable to do two years earlier – that violent upheavals, such as had taken place in France, were wholly undesirable.

The comparison with Wordsworth is especially relevant, as it has been suggested that in the *Letters from Sweden*, Wollstonecraft was anticipating some of the ideas of Romanticism (see Holmes (1987) pp. 39–41; Kelly (1992) pp. 187, 189). This is a claim which requires careful consideration. Certainly Wollstonecraft's desire to visit the unspoiled north of Norway – where, she has been told, the pure air and 'most romantic' countryside have cultivated extreme simplicity and honesty among the inhabitants, 'independence and virtue; affluence without vice; cultivation of the mind without depravity of the heart' (vi, p. 308) – is only one example of a recurring theme in the work: the beneficent effect of nature on the human heart. She says that it is essential to spend time alone in the countryside to develop knowledge, whether of ourselves or of others:

> in the country, growing intimate with nature, a thousand little circumstances . . . give birth to sentiments dear to the imagination, and inquiries which expand the soul . . . (vi, p. 256)

Although such passages could be said to point forward to Wordsworthian Romanticism – in the Preface to the *Lyrical Ballads* (1800), for example, Wordsworth wrote that in:

> low and rustic life . . . the essential passions of the heart find a better soil in which they can attain their maturity . . . in that situation the passions of men are incorporated with the beautiful and permanent forms of nature. (Wordsworth (1991) p. 245)

– Wollstonecraft's declaration clearly owes much to the influence of Rousseau and to eighteenth-century theories of landscape and the picturesque. But so, of course, did the stance of Wordsworth and his contemporaries. Eighteenth-century poets such as Thomson and Akenside wrote of the sublimity of nature and described its soothing or enlivening effects on the human psyche.[8] When Wollstonecraft abandons her narrative stance as neglected wife and constructs herself as a woman of strength and sensitivity for whom the beauties and sublimities of nature can mitigate the emotional pain she is suffering, she is, perhaps, simply following a relatively well-worn path:

> Rocks were piled on rocks, forming a suitable bulwark to the ocean . . . little patches of verdure, enamelled with the sweetest wild flowers, seemed to promise the goats and a few straggling cows luxurious herbage. How silent and peaceful was the scene. I gazed around with rapture, and felt more of that spontaneous pleasure which gives credibility to our expectations of happiness, than I had for a long, long time before . . . (vi, p. 247)

Where the later, Romantic, poets departed most radically from earlier theories of the sublime was in suggesting the possibility of the attainment of unity with the sublime object. Wordsworth and Coleridge both used the phrase 'One Life' to describe the posited subjective self and its identification with the objects of nature. They suggested that through the poetic imagination, especially in moments of solitude, this identification can become a tangible experience. This suggestion may also be found in *Letters from Sweden*:

> I was alone, till some involuntary sympathetic emotion, like the attraction of adhesion, made me feel that I was still a part of a mighty whole, from which I could not sever myself . . . (vi, p. 249)

Wollstonecraft's diction seems to allude to Pope's *Essay on Man*: 'All are but parts of one stupendous whole/Whose body Nature is, and God the Soul' (Epistle I, ll. 267–8), but although this is Pope at his most pre-Romantic, his lines lack the element of personal experience of oneness which characterises Wollstonecraft's description. This raises an interesting problem, since it is generally held that as a genre, the Romantic sublime is a masculine mode of writing. Women writers who enter its realm, according to Patricia Yaeger, 'contract to participate in a power struggle that, even when it is resisted, involves grim forces of possession and domination' (Yaeger (1989) p. 198). If the experience of the sublime, in the writings of male poets, enacts a moment of empowerment, then it is apparent that – in this passage, at least – Wollstonecraft differs in this respect. Her language begins by demonstrating more affinities with romantic novels than Romantic poetry – 'sympathetic emotion', 'attraction' – but ends with suggestions of entrapment – 'adhesion', 'I could not sever myself' – which assort oddly with the supposed optimism of the moment.

A later passage enacts another moment of sublimity:

> with what ineffable pleasure have I not gazed – and gazed again, losing my breath through my eyes – my very soul diffused itself in the scene – and, seeming to become all senses, glided in the scarcely-agitated waves, melted in the freshening breeze. (vi, p. 280)

As it stands, this passage seems to differ little from the 'male sublime' – Richard Holmes has suggested that it may have contributed to lines 39–44 of Coleridge's 'This Lime-Tree Bower my Prison' (1797) (Holmes (1987) pp. 38–9). In the continuation of the passage, however, Wollstonecraft describes herself as 'bow[ing] before the awful throne of my Creator, whilst I [rest] on its footstool' (*ibid.*), which some might read as an image of abasement, and which certainly has no counterpart in the Coleridge poem. It is also noticeable that she goes on, in the next paragraph, to exclaim that her heart has been 'chilled by sorrow and unkindness' (*ibid.*). This appears to make the passage into what Yaeger calls the 'failed sublime', in which 'a woman's dazzling, unexpected empowerment [is] followed by a moment in which this power is snatched away' (Yaeger (1989) p. 201); in this case the snatching is done by her memory of Imlay and his treatment of her.

In a recent Lacanian reading of *Letters from Sweden*, Jane Moore has argued that 'only in death . . . is it possible for a woman to imagine acquiring the plenitude of being which is the condition of the Lacanian imaginary and the *raison d'être* of the Romantic sublime' (Moore (1992) p. 149). It is certainly true that on Wollstonecraft's homeward journey, when she is noticeably more tired and depressed than she had been on setting out, her experiences of heightening of the imagination are coloured more and more by thoughts of death. Increasingly, the death of the body becomes the precondition for the liberation of the spirit. Walking through a pine grove on her way to view a waterfall, for example, she is struck by the 'grey cobweb-like appearance of the aged pines':

> the fibres whitening as they lose their moisture, imprisoned life seems to be stealing away. I cannot tell why – but death, under every form, appears to me like something getting free – to expand in I know not what element. (vi, p. 311)

The violence of the waterfall – '[t]he impetuous dashing of the rebounding torrent from the dark cavities' – produces a change to more 'tumultuous emotions', and she wonders briefly why she is 'chained to life and misery'. Even these reflections, however, are capable of being converted to a kind of pleasure, she says, as they lead her to thoughts of immortality and eternity: the only pleasure she can imagine is the release of death (*ibid.*). Earlier in the work, however, when her optimism is greater, she writes that not only can she not bear to think of death even though life may be excessively painful, but that:

> it appears to me impossible that I should cease to exist, or that this active, restless spirit, equally alive to joy and sorrow, should only be organized dust. . . . Surely something resides in the heart that is not perishable – and life is more than a dream. (vi, p. 281)

Jane Moore argues that 'there is no sense that Wollstonecraft's ego is strengthened by her experience' (Moore (1992) p. 153). But while this may perhaps be true of the particular passages she discusses (Letters Fifteen and Seventeen), elsewhere in the *Letters from Sweden* Wollstonecraft says that she values nature for its therapeutic, imaginative or spiritual effects. Like the Romantics, she places a high value on the imagination, which, she suggests, is enlivened by an appreciation of the natural world: 'Now all my nerves keep time with the melody of nature. . . . I must fly from thought, and find refuge from sorrow in a strong imagination . . .' (vi, p. 294). In Letter Nine, written from Tonsberg in Norway, she attributes to the involuntary exercise of the poetic imagination an experience in which she confers a form of consciousness on external nature, as Wordsworth was to do in *The Prelude* a few years later.[9] Passing through the pine groves in the evening, she writes, she has been 'struck with a mystic kind of reverence' – so much so that she has felt that the shadows are inhabited:

> I could scarcely conceive that they were without some consciousness of existence. . . . How often do my feelings remind me of the origin of many poetical fictions. In solitude, the imagination bodies forth its conceptions unrestrained, and stops enraptured to adore the beings of its own creation. These are moments of bliss; and the memory recalls them with delight. (vi, p. 286)[10]

Her religious sense, which never entirely deserts her, seems to be augmented by these experiences. Whatever soothes the senses of man, she argues, increases his devotion: even when we are unhappy, the beauties of nature are capable of reminding us of the blessings of existence – for the race, if not necessarily for her – which are in themselves a reminder of the creative role of God (vi, p. 307).

Wollstonecraft's optimism becomes less and less evident as the work progresses. Her depression becomes especially marked in the last few letters, in which she is passing through Germany on her way back to board her ship in Hamburg. As the personal letters show, she had received a packet of three of Imlay's letters in Gothenburg at the end of August, and another in Copenhagen on 6 September, which gave her 'fresh proofs of [his] indifference' (vi, pp. 425, 426), so that it became impossible for her to delude herself any longer that her exertions on his behalf had in any way endeared her to him again. Her profound despair at what she was returning to casts a blight over all she sees on the return journey: she finds the geography of the German heaths 'dreary' after the sublimities she has witnessed in Sweden and Norway, although she is favourably impressed with some of the towns (vi, p. 335). She is particularly depressed by the sight of a company of soldiers in Schleswig; they cause her to recall all the ideas she had previously held about 'german despotism'. Watching 'these beings trained to be sold to slaughter, or be slaughtered', she finds herself recalling 'an old opinion of mine':

> that it is the preservation of the species, not of individuals, which appears to be the design of the Deity throughout the whole of nature. Blossoms come forth only to be blighted; fish lay their spawn where it will be devoured; and what a large portion of the human race are born merely to be swept away. Does not this waste of budding life emphatically assert, that it is not men, but man, whose preservation is so necessary to the completion of the grand plan of the universe? (vi, p. 336)

Her final letter is bleak, and cut short to indicate that she has also cut her journey short – she did not visit Germany more extensively, or Switzerland, as she intended. She has had enough of travelling, she writes, and the Dover cliffs seem to her insignificant compared to the sights she has seen in Scandinavia – her 'spirit of observation seems to be fled'. She herself seems numbed, diminished like the white cliffs, and fearful of a different kind of journey into a different kind of territory, though more unknown and frightening in its way – to rejection, humiliation and death. The final image in the *Letters from Sweden* is one of her wandering desolately round 'this dirty town', too full of unhappy and intrusive thoughts to do more than prepare for her journey back to London (vi, p. 345). The narrative continues, however, in the 'Letters to Imlay', with her suicide note, written about a week after her arrival in England: 'I write to you now on my knees; imploring you to send my child and the nurse . . . to Paris. . . . Let the maid have all my clothes, without distinction . . .' (vi, p. 430); her 'lament, that, when the bitterness of death was past, I was inhumanly brought back to life and misery' (vi, p. 431); and her gradual recuperation, and slow progress to the point where she is able to say her 'eternal farewell' (vi, p. 438) – not, according to Godwin, until March 1796 (Holmes (1987) p. 254).

As Godwin suggests, it is a tribute to her intelligence and her professionalism that during this period of profound 'mental torture' (Holmes (1987) p. 255) she nevertheless completed the *Letters from Sweden*, and prepared it for the press.

Chapter 7

◆

The Wrongs of Woman; or, Maria (1798)

According to Godwin, Wollstonecraft was engaged in the composition of *The Wrongs of Woman* 'for more than twelve months before her decease' (Holmes (1987) p. 264), and this is borne out by the few references to the work which can be found in her letters. She seems to have sent Godwin a revised version of the manuscript to read on 21 July 1796 (Wardle (1979) p. 331); and again on 26 August 1796, wanting encouragement, she sent him perhaps another version (Wardle (1979) p. 342). By 4 September she has been thrown into a 'depression of spirits' by Godwin's criticism of her manner of writing – he seems to have said, or implied, 'that there was a radical defect in it'. She has not been able to continue with her book; since he saw the manuscript 'I have scarce written a word to please myself' (Wardle (1979) pp. 344–5). She makes a determined defence of her writings as having 'more mind' than other people's, but has obviously been entirely deflated by Godwin's criticism. Her reaction was, it seems, excessive, because Godwin's response not only reassured her but persuaded her to accept grammar lessons from him, although it is not altogether plain why he thought she needed them. On 15 September she looks forward to her lesson with him, even if she hopes it will be combined with dalliance (Wardle (1979) p. 381). Since she and Godwin were in continuous contact from that date until her death, it is reasonable to suppose that the novel continued to be a topic of conversation between them, and that they discussed her revisions and her progress with the work. His own practice as an author was, presumably, available to her, but there is little evidence that she really profited from it.

In May 1797, Wollstonecraft gave the manuscript to Godwin's friend George Dyson to read. It is hard to know what exactly Dyson said about the novel: only Wollstonecraft's reply to his letter has survived. Godwin quoted from this only partially in his introduction to the novel in *Posthumous Works*, and it is interesting to see what he left out (Wardle (1979) pp. 391–2; i, pp. 83–4). Among the passages he omitted was one in which she describes herself as 'vexed and surprised' by the fact that Dyson had not been sufficiently moved by Maria's plight; she can account for this lack of 'delicacy of feeling' only by the fact that Dyson is a man. Godwin also removed the exclamation which shows that she felt, presumably for the same reason, that Dyson was too indulgent to the husband: 'yet you do not seem to be disgusted with him!!!'. In fact, the only two people she allowed to read the manuscript were male, but presumably she hoped that they would show more delicate feelings than she attributed to the ordinary run of men. She says at the beginning of the letter that she has found his remarks 'discouraging', but this apparently means not that she feels she has failed to do what she set out to do but, rather, that the failure is his: 'I am not satisfied with the feelings that seem to be the result of the perusal'. Despite the defensive tone of this letter, however, she was obviously dissatisfied with the work. Godwin's description of the composition sounds like a painful struggle, which presumably owed something to his own and Dyson's critical comments:

> All her other works were produced with a rapidity, that did not give her powers time fully to expand. But this was written slowly and with mature consideration. She began it in several forms, which she successively rejected, after they were considerably advanced. She wrote many parts of the work again and again and, when she had finished what she intended for the first part, she felt herself more urgently stimulated to revise and improve what she had written, than to proceed, with constancy of application, in the parts that were to follow. (Holmes (1987) p. 264)

Godwin testifies to Wollstonecraft's determination to make *The Wrongs of Woman* a 'truly excellent novel'; none the less, it is hard to see how it ever would have been good enough to have satisfied her rigorous critical standards. In her reviewing for the *Analytical* she had expressed her disappointment at the triviality and sentimentality of the majority of contemporary fiction, and had been quick to appreciate that which was good. She was determined that her novel would be serious, a powerful indictment of society's oppression of women which would be a call for change in the laws and in the community's attitudes, so that if the novel outlined the position of woman as it is, the reforms it initiated might effect the position of woman as it ought to be. But her sense of the realities of the situation overcame the need for her fiction to gather imaginative conviction as well as reforming force, and her indignation at the outrage committed on woman in the name of society subdued her detachment and closed, fatally, the distance between herself and her characters, between the author and her fiction. These fragments – *The Wrongs of Woman* is far from being a complete work – demonstrate the strength of Wollstonecraft's mind and the integrity of her convictions. They also demonstrate her acute, often dazzling insight into her own personality and motives; it is these autobiographical passages that many modern readers will value most.

It has been suggested that *The Wrongs of Woman* was intended to show the society which had produced the system she had tried to reform in *Rights of Woman*, and that the two works bear the same relation as Godwin's *Caleb Williams* and *Political Justice*. It is not at all certain that this is the case; but if it were, her reasons for choosing to continue her arguments in the form of a novel are not difficult to find. The novel of ideas was a relatively new and extremely popular genre, and some literary English radicals in the circle to which Wollstonecraft belonged were using the form to disseminate their philosophical theories.

A number of female novelists, especially those who shared Wollstonecraft's political beliefs, had published such works. Elizabeth Inchbald (1753–1831), actress, translator and playwright, published *A Simple Story* (1791) and *Nature and Art* (1796), both of which deal, albeit in differing ways, with the subject of the effect of education on the character and moral development. The same subject also forms the theme of Eliza Fenwick's *Secresy; or, The Ruin on the Rock* (1795), which, in its description of the confinement in a castle of one of its heroines, may have suggested Wollstonecraft's use of a similar idea in *The Wrongs of Woman*, although this was, of course, a popular Gothic device. Mary Hays (1760–1843), with whom Wollstonecraft became friends in 1796, used her relationship with the

Cambridge thinker William Frend and her correspondence with
Godwin, as well as other frankly autobiographical material, in her
Memoirs of Emma Courtney (1796): the autobiography, and the fact
that the novel claimed a woman's right to acknowledge her own
passionate feelings without any previous declaration by the man,
caused something of a scandal to be associated with this work, and
with its author. Charlotte Smith (1749–1806), apparently known to
Wollstonecraft only through her prolific writings, wrote in support
of the French Revolution in *Desmond* (1792), and criticised the part
played by the British government in the American War of
Independence in *The Old Manor House* (1794). None of these works,
however, contains anything approaching the consistently political
feminism of *The Wrongs of Woman*.

Among the best-known male Jacobin novelists of the period were
Robert Bage (1720–1801), whose *Hermsprong; or Man as He is Not*
(1796) Wollstonecraft praised in the *Analytical* for its 'strength of
mind and frankness of heart' (vii, pp. 477–8); Thomas Holcroft
(1745–1809), a close associate of Godwin and, later, of Wollstonecraft, who wrote approvingly of his *Anna St Ives* (1792) in the
Analytical (vii, pp. 439–41); and, of course, Godwin himself.
Wollstonecraft borrowed the second volume of *Caleb Williams* from
him in February 1797. She may have been interested in the prison
scene, although the pursuit of Maria by her husband seems to owe
something to the example of Godwin's novel.

Wollstonecraft was, of course, familiar with a number of Gothic
novels – during the period when she was composing *The Wrongs of
Woman* she reviewed, with qualifed approval, Ann Radcliffe's *The
Italian* (1796) (vii, pp. 484–5) – from which she may have derived
some of the themes of imprisonment and madness which she uses in
The Wrongs of Woman. Finally, of course, she had any number of anti-
models, as her astringent reviews from the early days of the *Analytical*
make abundantly clear. In addition, she expressed a profound
dissatisfaction with her own earlier attempt at novel writing,
describing *Mary* in a letter to her sister Everina on 22 March 1797 as
'a crude production' (Wardle (1979) p. 385).

The ideas which *The Wrongs of Woman* sets out to disseminate are
chiefly developments of the thinking in the *Rights of Woman*. The
work also contains more general social comment, in its criticism of
institutions such as hospitals and workhouses, and social evils such as
the practice of impressment, all of which Wollstonecraft had written

about in earlier works. Also, particularly in the section which gives an account of Jemima's life history, the novel contains material which illustrates the effect of education and environment on the development of the moral character, a theme which had always interested Wollstonecraft. In this, and in the sections which assert that human beings are capable of improvement if they meet with the right conditions, Wollstonecraft was no doubt encouraged by her association with Godwin: these are themes which are important both to his *Political Justice* and to *Caleb Williams*.

The Wrongs of Woman, even in its unfinished state, is a much less sentimental work than *Mary*. It is also more sophisticated, both structurally and philosophically. The structure is complex. The book begins with its heroine, Maria, gradually regaining consciousness to find herself a prisoner in a madhouse, a horrifying 'mansion of despair' in which the 'groans and shrieks' of her unseen companions mingle with her own confused memories of her past life to produce a 'whirlwind of rage and indignation' over which she only gradually gains control (i, p. 85). As the novel develops, Maria's life story is gradually unfolded for the reader – partly by her own revelations in the dramatic present, and later, in much greater detail, by means of a long written account which she prepares for her daughter to read in later life. In addition, the work contains the stories of other women's lives: most notably that of Maria's jailor, Jemima, but also those of several other women from the labouring class.

This multiplicity of women's life stories shows women united by the wrongs which a male-dominated society imposes on them. As well as its overt didacticism, the novel works on a metaphorical level, as Wollstonecraft herself makes clear in her Preface, in which she says that her desire to exhibit 'the misery and oppression, peculiar to women, that arise out of the partial laws and customs of society' has 'restrained her fancy', so that the story should be considered to be that of 'woman' rather than of an individual (i, p. 83). Thus, not only does Maria's initial imprisonment represent the condition of women in general, as she herself is made to acknowledge: 'Was not the world a vast prison, and women born slaves' (i, p. 88), but the novel's other paradigmatic female lives – one woman forced into prostitution by economic necessity, another shown to be powerless to resist the tyranny of her husband, a third who advocates submission to men for the sake of a quiet life – not only represent individual cases of social and legal injustice but also, on a deeper level, work as metaphors for sexual, economic and psychological debasement.

The emphasis which Wollstonecraft places in her Preface on the legal injustices under which women are made to suffer is most fully worked out in the main story, that of Maria's attempts to escape not only from her prison but also from the confines of her disastrous marriage. At the beginning the reader learns that Maria has been separated from her child – a fact which is used later as a sharp indictment of the existing marriage laws – but it is only at the end of the first volume that Wollstonecraft reveals the details of her heroine's injudicious and unhappy marriage. In doing so, incidentally, she illustrates one of the important arguments of the *Rights of Woman*: the ill-judged, sentimental attachment which Maria develops for the man she later marries is shown to have been a result of her narrow education, and of the fact that she had taken refuge from an unhappy childhood in reading romantic novels. As a result, when she first meets George Venables, she invests him with 'more than mortal beauty. My fancy had found a basis to erect its model of perfection on . . .' (i, p. 131). Unfortunately, by the time Maria discovers the flaws in her husband's character – he is a libertine, and also quickly runs through the money which she has brought to the marriage – it is too late: 'I had been caught in a trap, and caged for life' (i, p. 138).

One of the most painful results of this situation for Maria is the fact that although Venables becomes increasingly physically repugnant to her as a result of his drinking and his extra-marital indulgences, which are 'entirely promiscuous, and of the most brutal nature' (i, p. 139), she is still expected to submit to his sexual demands, because women are regarded by society as their husbands' property. In its frank discussion of sexuality, *The Wrongs of Woman* differs substantially from the latent puritanism of the *Rights of Woman*. One of Wollstonecraft's boldest passages in the novel – and one which requires a determined exercise of the historical imagination by the twentieth-century reader if its contemporary shock value is to be fully appreciated – is that in which Maria asserts a woman's right to sexual fulfilment. Particularly notable is the way in which Wollstonecraft associates the ability to respond sexually with the imagination, which in turn is viewed as the foundation of '*positive* virtue':

When novelists or moralists praise as a virtue, a woman's coldness of constitution, and want of passion; and make her yield to her lover out of sheer compassion, or to promote a frigid plan of future comfort, I am disgusted. They may be good women, in the ordinary acceptation of the phrase, and do no harm; but they appear not to have those 'finely fashioned nerves' which render the senses exquisite. They may possess tenderness, but they want that fire of the imagination, which produces *active* sensibility, and *positive* virtue . . . we cannot, without depraving our minds, endeavour to please a lover or husband, but in proportion as he pleases us. (i, pp. 144–5)

The fact that, feeling as she does, she has nevertheless sacrificed her principles and submitted herself sexually to Venables, becoming pregnant as a result, causes Maria to reflect, with extreme shame, on the double standard which prevails in her society. No one, she argues, would expect a man to continue to love a woman who had succumbed to alcoholism, or judge him harshly if he fell in love with another woman; but women are expected to devote their lives to a dissipated, intemperate spendthrift, and allowed no recourse to more congenial company (i, p. 145). Maria describes herself as having resisted, as a result of her own high principles, the temptation offered by the flattery of various male admirers, although she suggests that she now (that is, in the dramatic present of the novel) views such principles as 'prejudices at war with nature and reason' (i, p. 147) – a suggestion borne out by the development of her relationship with Darnford.

Maria's sympathetic uncle, an advanced thinker, encourages her developing resolve to separate from Venables, telling her that he is 'far from thinking that a woman, once married, ought to consider the engagement as indissoluble . . . in case her husband merits neither her love, nor her esteem' (i, p. 147). Maria, however, is crucially aware that her legal position is an impossible one: as a married woman she has become one of the '*out-laws* of the world' (i, p. 146). She laments the fact that since her husband has never inflicted physical harm on her, she lacks the only admissible grounds for divorce:

a wife being as much a man's property as his horse or his ass, she has nothing she can call her own. . . . The tender mother cannot *lawfully* snatch from the gripe of the gambling spendthrift, or beastly drunkard, unmindful of his offspring, the fortune which falls to her by chance; or (so flagrant is the injustice) what she earns by her own exertions. No; he can rob her with impunity, even to waste publicly on a courtezan; and the laws of her own country – if women have a country – afford her no protection or redress from the oppressor, unless she have the plea of bodily fear . . . (i, p. 149)

She finally musters the courage to leave Venables when she discovers that he has arranged a loan from an acquaintance in return for her own sexual favours. Venables pursues her relentlessly from lodging to lodging, and at last, after the birth of her daughter, she decides to move to the Continent to begin a new life. But Venables buys off the maid she has hired to accompany her on the journey, and she is drugged, robbed of her child, and incarcerated in the madhouse.

Thus much of Maria's story is told in flashback, in the 'memoirs' she writes during her imprisonment, which offer her some temporary relief from her tormenting thoughts as well as the possibility of future instruction for her daughter (i, p. 90). The story continues in the dramatic present of the novel, with Maria's developing relationship with her fellow captive Henry Darnford bringing additional complexity to the unfolding of events. At the end of the existing completed portion of the work, she has escaped from the asylum to set up home with her lover, and has been snubbed by several ladies of her former acquaintance, giving her cause to reflect on the double standards practised in a society which would have condoned her remaining with her husband while taking a lover, but refuses to acknowledge her right to do so openly (i, p. 176). No doubt this reflection owed much to the fact that Wollstonecraft had experienced something of this double standard in her own life: after her marriage to Godwin, several of her female acquaintances refused to continue to acknowledge her socially, on the grounds that marrying Godwin had proved that she had not been married to Imlay. Venables discovers their whereabouts, and brings an action against Darnford for seduction and adultery. Maria decides to undertake his defence herself, and the final completed chapter is chiefly devoted to her impassioned speech in court.

Her plea is based on a radical reinterpretation of moral standards. She appeals not to the law, or to the judge, but to the jury; and to history over the heads of both. She stands for humanity and decency, and against existing institutions. She contrasts the laws imposed by 'the policy of an artificial society' with a woman's absolute prerogative to 'consult her conscience, and regulate her conduct . . . by her own sense of right' (i, p. 180). The unprincipled conduct of Venables has ensured that she will never again be able to regard him as a husband, and she has long believed herself 'in the sight of heaven, free' (i, p. 181), and thus at liberty to form a new tie. She pleads for a divorce, so that she may marry Darnford: as the reader has learnt earlier, she is prepared to marry despite her view that the present social constitution of marriage leads to immorality, since she wishes 'to avow her affection to Darnford, by becoming his wife, according to established rules' (i, p. 177). The chapter ends with the judge's summary dismissal of Maria's plea in terms which underline once again how far society needs to progress before it can recognise the justice of her arguments:

> We did not want French principles in public or private life – and, if women were allowed to plead their feelings, as an excuse or palliation of infidelity, it was opening a floodgate for immorality. What virtuous woman thought of her feelings? – It was her duty to love and obey the man chosen by her parents and relations, who were qualified by their experience to judge better for her, than she could for herself. (i, p. 181)

Maria's relationship with Darnford represents the major problem for readers of *The Wrongs of Woman*: as the novel stands in its unfinished state, it is not clear precisely what status Wollstonecraft meant to accord it. On the one hand – presumably influenced by the 'friendship melting into love' (Holmes (1987) p. 258) which was developing between herself and Godwin – she seems to want to show a steady growth of rational but genuine affection, eventually leading to a physical consummation which constitutes a marriage in all but name: 'As her husband she now received him, and he solemnly pledged himself as her protector – and eternal friend' (i, p. 173). On the other hand, as hints elsewhere in the novel seem to indicate, and as the several – and uniformly unhappy – projected endings confirm, Wollstonecraft appears to have intended to show that Maria's trust in Darnford proves as misplaced as her trust in her husband had been; instead of the fulfilment for which she so confidently hopes, the conclusions draw on Wollstonecraft's own experience of life, figuring in various forms desertion, suicide attempts, miscarriages and withdrawals into selfless maternal devotion (i, p. 182–3).

If Maria's story broadens the arguments of the *Rights of Woman* by addressing the legal position of women within marriage, the life history of Maria's jailor, Jemima, a woman of the labouring class, also goes beyond the confines of that earlier work, in which she had explicitly stated in her Introduction: 'I pay particular attention to those in the middle class' (v, p. 75). Jemima's story demonstrates, in a number of ways, the evils which result from the existing state of society. Jemima's birth and early childhood illustrate the situation described in the *Rights of Woman* where an oppressed woman becomes an oppressor of her own inferiors, as well as providing an example of society's double standards where men and women are concerned. Jemima's mother, a young servant girl who had been seduced by a fellow employee, had died nine days after her birth, neglected by her 'virtuous mistress', who 'felt no sympathy for the poor wretch, denied any comfort required by her situation', although her father was only mildly reproved, and allowed to continue in his employment (i, p. 107). The baby is farmed out to the cheapest wet nurse available, a woman whose heart has been hardened by poverty and deprivation so that she, in her turn, has no love or tenderness to pass on to the children in her care. Neither here nor in the home which her father later grudgingly offers her, when his new wife suggests that another pair of hands might be useful around the house, does Jemima receive any love or affection, and Wollstonecraft makes an unequivocal connection between this fact and the child's stunted physical and moral development:

> Left in dirt, to cry with cold and hunger till I was weary, and sleep without ever being prepared by exercise, or lulled by kindness to rest; could I be expected to become any thing but a weak and rickety babe? Still, in spite of neglect, I continued to exist, to learn to curse existence . . . and the treatment that rendered me miserable, seemed to sharpen my wits. (i, pp. 107–8)

Neglected, and abused both physically and mentally by her father, stepmother and half-sister, Jemima quickly learns to lie and steal as a means of self-preservation. Looking back, she attributes most of the misery she suffered to the lack of a mother's affection: 'I was, in fact, born a slave, and chained by infamy to slavery during the whole of existence' (i, p. 110). At the age of 16 she is raped by the man she works for, and thrown out of the house by his wife when she discovers them together. She aborts the child she is carrying, and turns to prostitution as the only viable means of supporting herself. Dragged on to an even lower level of society than the one where she had started her life, she finds that she is still 'a slave, a bastard, a common property' (i, p. 112). After some time of this unsatisfactory life, which she nevertheless values for the small amount of independence it offers, she decides to accept a place in a house of ill fame, tired of being exploited by the town watchmen, who:

> not content with receiving from us, outlaws of society . . . a brutal gratification gratuitously as a privilege of office . . . exort a tithe of

prostitution, and harass with threats the poor creatures whose occupation affords not the means to silence the growl of avarice. (i, p. 113)[1]

In this new and comparatively sheltered situation her health improves, and even her manners improve, partly as a result of the need to become more refined in order to attract clients, but also because, in direct contrast to her earlier experience of life: 'I was not shut out from all intercourse of humanity' (i, p. 113). Her moral education really begins when she accepts an offer to become the housekeeper, and kept mistress, of an elderly gentleman. In his house she has access to books and to the company of educated men, and gradually acquires 'new principles', on the basis of which she begins to have aspirations to establish herself as a respectable member of society (i, p. 114). After the sudden death of her protector, however, she again finds herself destitute: his family order her to leave the house and refuse to give her references, so that she is unable to find alternative employment. In desperation she writes to one of the gentlemen whom she has met at her protector's house, appealing for help. His reply illustrates the fact that he, in common with most of his peers, is in total ignorance of the real conditions prevailing in society. Ironically, it is Jemima's newly acquired literacy and her intelligence which now militate against her: a woman who could compose such a letter, he writes:

> could never be in want of resources, were she to look into herself, and exert her powers; misery was the consequence of indolence, and, as to my being shut out from society, it was the lot of man to submit to certain privations. (i, p. 115)

Jemima comments that the assertion that work can be found by anyone willing to exert themselves to look for it is a fallacy as far as women are concerned; even hard manual labour is denied to many women who are deemed to have lost their reputation (i, pp. 115–16). She finally succeeds in finding work as a washerwoman for a few families who are prepared to turn a blind eye to her less than respectable past in return for hard labour 'from one in the morning till eight at night, for eighteen or twenty pence a day' (i, p. 116). In the misery and desperation which result from this mechanical slavery, she accepts an offer to become the mistress of a tradesman: 'Consider, madam, that I was famishing: wonder not that I became a wolf!'

(i, p. 117). Hardened by her recent experiences, she advises him to turn out a young servant girl whom he has made pregnant. He does so, and the girl drowns herself: Jemima herself witnesses the scene the next morning, when the body is discovered, and determines not to live with the man (*ibid.*). She injures her leg in an accident with a washtub, and although she is in desperate need of medical attention she has to wait several weeks for admission to a hospital because she lacks a recommendation from the 'rich and respectable', and cannot afford the fees they demand. Even after she is finally admitted, she is discharged before her leg has properly healed because she cannot pay the money demanded for washing her linen so that she will appear 'decently' when the surgeon visits the hospital:

> I cannot give you an adequate idea of the wretchedness of an hospital; everything is left to the care of people intent on gain. The attendants seem to have lost all compassion in the bustling discharge of their offices. . . . Everything appeared to be conducted for the accommodation of the medical men and their pupils, who came to make experiments on the poor, for the benefit of the rich. (i, p. 118)[2]

Dismissed from the hospital, unable to work because of her injury, Jemima develops a hatred of mankind and, convincing herself that the rich and poor are natural enemies, becomes a thief 'from principle'. She is arrested and imprisoned for six months; then, after she is turned out into the streets penniless, she collapses and is sent to a workhouse, one of any number of such 'wretched asylums', which Jemima compares to prisons, 'in which many respectable old people, worn out by immoderate labour, sink into the grave in sorrow, to which they are carried like dogs!' (i, pp. 118–19). She is rescued by the overseer who, noticing the evidence of some resolution in her manner, offers her forty pounds a year to take charge of the madhouse where Maria is incarcerated.

Clearly Jemima's story is intended to illustrate not only specific social evils such as those of the hospital and the workhouse but also more fundamental principles which were held by Wollstonecraft and, no doubt, reinforced by Godwin: that education and environment have a profound effect on the development of the moral character. Furthermore, she serves as an illustration of the belief that, given suitable conditions, all human beings are susceptible of improvement. We discover from Jemima's own account that her principles and character improve substantially during the period when she is in contact with more cultured minds, at the house of her protector. In addition, as the novel goes on to describe, her humanity has 'rather been benumbed than killed' by the painful experiences of her life (i, p. 120), and the kindness of Maria, as well as the example of her selfless love for her lost child, reawaken her capacity to feel, so that by the end of the existing text she has become Maria's devoted attendant and friend (i, pp. 174–5).

Another criticism which George Dyson made of the novel concerned the style of Jemima's story. Wollstonecraft's response indicates that he felt Jemima's language was not appropriate to her working-class origins – she suggested that he was confounding 'simplicity with vulgarity', although she was willing to reconsider this point (Wardle (1979) p. 392). Nevertheless, it is hard to demonstrate that Jemima's style is in any way individualised by either simplicity or vulgarity: it is, in fact, little different from that of Maria. Her narrative is not characterised by idiomatic or dialectal particularities; there is little localised or linguistic life in it. Her description of the child's despair is given in stilted, literary language, full of qualifications:

> sullen pride, or a kind of stupid desperation, made me, at length, almost regardless of contempt, which had wrung from me so many solitary tears, at the only moments when I was allowed to rest. (i, p. 110)

As for Jemima's reaction to the effects of rape, physical violence, and the discovery that she is pregnant:

> The anguish which was now pent up in my bosom, seemed to open a new world to me: I began to extend my thoughts beyond myself, and grieve for human misery, until I discovered, with horror – ah! what horror! – that I was with child. (i, p. 110)

This description lacks actuality; it does not carry conviction. The misery and horror it proclaims – 'horror – ah! what horror!' – hardly amount to dramatic realisation either remembered or re-enacted. Jemima's narration is quite as literary as that of Maria, and in neither case can the narrator be confidently separated from the author. Wollstonecraft had little or no gift for reproducing speech rhythms or conversations. She seldom presents characters speaking together, engaged in argument or even in cordiality. She always has her characters tell their own stories and thus, as author, stays in sole charge of the narration. The life and culture of the lower classes, with all their squalor and their vitality, would have been presented in the speech of Jemima, without the intervention of the author and the decorum of literary precedents. Jemima's story may well have been modelled, in some respects, on that of Moll Flanders, but in Moll's style, unlike Jemima's, the rhythms of the narrative follow the rhythms of speech; the diction is concrete and direct, reflecting the world of things in which Moll lives and is entrapped, and where the references are an index of the practical, day-to-day life of one whose main object is merely to survive in a world that threatens her existence. Moll learns the same lessons as Jemima, and both endorse the view that morality is a luxury they cannot afford. Concepts of right and wrong are for those who do not have to worry continually about where their next meal is coming from. Morality, in fact, can be established only where there is economic security, and women in Jemima's position have few ways of obtaining that. But so far as the style of her narration is concerned, it would be interesting to know how the discussion between Wollstonecraft and Dyson went when they met for tea in order to go over it (Wardle (1979) p. 392).

Other subsidiary episodes in the novel serve to draw attention to further flaws in the existing social system and in the prevailing relations between the sexes. Peggy, a poor woman of Maria's acquaintance, suffers loneliness and hardship after her husband is pressed into the navy against his will, and subsequently killed in his first engagement with the enemy. Maria learns that Peggy is unable to afford to put her children out to nurse and unwilling to hand them over to the care of the parish, and sets her up in a little shop. But she is forced to take in washing to supplement her income, and the theft (by a recruiting party) of a large amount of clothing leads to her goods being seized by her inhuman landlord in lieu of the rent, which she has become unable to pay (i, pp. 127–9).

Later, during her flight from Venables, Maria encounters two landladies, both of whom illustrate the degrading and unjust conditions which women have to suffer. The first deplores Maria's decision to leave her husband, since she believes that 'when a woman was once married, she must bear every thing' (i, p. 158). She works from morning till night to support her drunken husband, who nevertheless robs the till and spends the money she has kept to pay the bills, and beats her when he comes home drunk. Despite this treatment, however, she is devoted to her 'dear Johnny', and will do anything to win a few words of kindness from him: his 'thawed sternness, contrasted with his habitual brutality, was the more acceptable, and could not be purchased at too dear a rate' (i, p. 160).

Maria's second landlady has also suffered at the hands of man and of society. She too believes that 'Women must be submissive', although she has been brought to the brink of destitution by a bad husband who has pawned all her clothes and goods, and spent the money on a kept mistress: when she goes to the pawnbroker and offers to take an oath that the goods are hers, however, she is told: '"It was all one, my husband had a right to whatever I had"' (i, p. 164). She has worked hard to re-establish herself in the world, and is anxious about the risk involved in helping Maria – she knows too well '"that women have always the worst of it, when the law is to decide"' (i, p. 165).

Godwin's Afterword to the existing portion of the novel raises the question of whether the 'hints' left by Wollstonecraft of her plan for the conclusion would, in fact, have filled very many more additional pages. His argument, however, is that the strength of Wollstonecraft's work lay not in the creation of a multiplicity of incidents but in her capacity to:

> develop events, to discover their capabilities, to ascertain the different passions and sentiments with which they are fraught, and to diversify them with incidents, that give reality to the picture . . . (i, p. 184)

The very fact that he raised the problem in the first place seems to suggest the possibility that he shared some of the anxieties he set out to allay. Perhaps this is not entirely surprising – a novel of ideas must still be a novel, and not become a tract, and it is arguable whether Wollstonecraft achieved – or ever would have achieved – this. Her response to Dyson's criticism – 'I am not satisfied with the feelings which seem to be the result of the perusal' (Wardle (1979) p. 391) – suggests that she was unable to distinguish the story she tells, with all its pathos and suffering, from her presentation of that story which, for the most part, is reflective and abstract. After all, it was her business as a novelist to evoke disgust from the reader in the way she dramatised the story, but she does not, in fact, really dramatise it at all – it is told in indirect speech, for the most part from Maria's point of view. Wollstonecraft mixes the telling of the story with extended commentary on it and its implications for women in general in order to turn the particular experience into a general problem, one woman's sufferings standing in for the sufferings of the sex as a whole, as she says herself in the Preface. However effective this may or may not be as a way of highlighting the wrongs of womankind, it is also a way of dissipating what immediacy and conflict there is in the tale as a presentation of an individual marriage.

In this context, it is worth quoting in full her response to Godwin's criticism of her writing:

> I am compelled to think that there is some thing in my writings more valuable, than in the productions of some people on whom you bestow warm eulogiums – I mean more mind – denominate it as you will – more observations of my own senses, more of the combining of my own imagination – the effusions of my own feelings and passions than the cold workings of the brain on the materials procured by the senses and imagination of other writers. (Wardle (1979) p. 345)

Putting aside her sense of injured merit – since Godwin had criticised her writings – it is clear that she prides herself on her ability to combine the intellect and the imagination with the power of fancy and passion, in a phraseology which would not have seemed out of place in Wordsworth's Preface to the *Lyrical Ballads*. All the elements are in place for a Romantic work of fiction, which she sadly fails to achieve. This failure is certainly not due to any lack of intellect, or of feelings and passion; it is a thorough-going failure of imagination. She fails to sustain the world of her fiction as an independent imaginative structure – it is undermined by a relentless didacticism in which everything combines to support her thesis, but does not adhere as an organic fiction. She was more interested in indicting society for its persecution of women than she was in presenting and dramatising that society and the women in it. She never really understood the difference between dramatisation and theatricality, between presenting character and editorialising on it.

Gary Kelly has written of Godwin's and Wollstonecraft's fiction that 'autobiography is the central form . . . because in one's self are written the evils of "things as they are" and the institutionalized "wrongs of woman"' (Kelly (1989) p. 41). But while Godwin's own life experiences are largely separate from those of his fictional characters – at least in *Caleb Williams* – Wollstonecraft's constantly intrude, to the detriment of her fiction. Nothing is really allowed to have independent life, especially not the projection of herself and her own experiences – she is too busy trying to understand them. In addition, as Mary Poovey has pointed out, she never fully separates her own values from the values of the social institutions which she condemns, to the detriment of her political argument (Poovey (1984) p. 96).

Her portrait – an anatomy of society rather than an imaginative re-creation of it – is fuelled by personal experience, peopled by ghosts of her past and addressed to women of the future, particularly with her daughter in mind. In this she may have been thinking of her friend Marie Roland, who left France's future in the hands of her daughter, but it is strange and ironic that it was left to her own daughter, another Mary, who kept her mother's works by her at all times, to write the most accomplished of all Romantic novels, whose social implications were profound but which, being largely fantasy, had little factual and no political basis in fact at all. Marie Roland was executed by the Revolution in which she had invested her faith and her values, only to be betrayed by the men in her life and by the enemies within herself: sensibility, truth, and the need to trust and love. Wollstone-craft had been similarly betrayed: she had projected her wishes on to the world, she had invested her hopes in Imlay, she had been misguided by her own desires and deluded by her own feelings to believe that the world – and Imlay – returned her thoughts and feelings. But it – and he – only mirrored herself: she saw her own reflection and thought it was the world – and him. Her disillusion motivates the unrelieved harshness of her analysis of women in society; her illusion saves her from bitterness, but removes her from immediate experience. Behind all the men – particularly Venables and, more nakedly, the Darnford of the unwritten Part III – lies the betrayer Imlay; and all the women are related to Wollstonecraft or her immediate family.

Godwin, in differentiating between the relative strengths of the sexes, claims logical thought and intellectual curiosity for himself, and attributes intuition and imagination to women, including Wollstonecraft (Holmes (1987) p. 272). Yet in this novel there is a distinct lack of intuition and imagination, especially in Wollstone-craft's refusal to allow her characters a life of their own – but a good deal of evidence of thought and intellection. The novel becomes a nightmare of suffering and oppression developed against the background of male tyranny operating through the machinery of law and society to force women to accept their dependency with servility. But it is the facts and her arguments that prevail, not any imaginative vision that another novel might well have drawn from them. She attacks impressment of unwilling men into the navy as a means of recruitment as she had done in the *Rights of Men*, though she now centres her concern on its repercussions on the family. Peggy's destitution makes the evils of impressment more real, yet if her sufferings are real, Peggy herself lacks imaginative credibility.

In the *Analytical*, reviewing a pamphlet by B. Faulkner, *Observations on the general and improper treatment of insanity* (vii, p. 236), Wollstonecraft had stressed the importance of the subject, and insisted that the length of the extract she printed needed no apology. In particular she had supported Faulkner's attack on doctors who locked up those suffering from mental illness, removing them from their homes and debarring them from the attentions of their friends. Maria's imprisonment is fully realised allegorically, but lacks the profound reality of that anarchy Wollstonecraft describes so vividly in presenting the insanity of the king in the *Rights of Men*, or the impotent rage with which she sympathises in her review of Faulkner's pamphlet. However important socially Wollstonecraft may consider these matters, they fail to achieve that animation that fiction usually confers on the concrete and abstract when they are touched with the light of creativity. Like her earlier attempt – albeit on a grander and more ambitious scale – *The Wrongs of Woman* cannot be called anything but a failure as it stands. Nevertheless, whatever her technical inexperience, she would, given time, have mastered the craft of fiction and learnt the necessary disciplines for turning the life of the self into the material of the novelist's art.

Chapter 8

◆

'On Poetry, and Our Relish for the Beauties of Nature' (1797) 'Hints (Chiefly Designed to have been incorporated in the Second Part of the Vindication of the Rights of Woman)' [1798]

The Essay on Poetry, which was first published – as a letter to the editor – in the *Monthly Magazine* in April 1797 (vol. iii, pp. 279–82), is the only piece of literary theory Wollstonecraft ever produced. It represents a crystallisation of ideas about creativity and the poetic imagination which she had touched on in a number of reviews, as well as a development of the interest she had expressed in the human response to nature in the *Letters from Sweden*. There are also a number of related passages which Godwin included in *Posthumous Works* as nos. 22–31 of 'Hints (Chiefly Designed to have been incorporated in the Second Part of the Vindication of the Rights of Woman)' (v, pp. 274–6).

The status of 'Hints' is something of a mystery, and the title is obviously a mistake. For one thing, they are not 'Hints' but 'Aphorisms'; for another, they are obviously not designed to be incorporated in the second part of the *Rights of Woman*. Some of the aphorisms are on women, some are on art, most are on other things. But the writing of aphorisms was not at all uncommon, especially on the Continent: La Rochefoucauld's *Maxims* (which Wollstonecraft had read in Ireland in 1787) were the most famous. But so far as England, and particularly Wollstonecraft, were concerned, the fashion for aphorism was probably furthered by Fuseli's translation of *Aphorisms on Man: translated from the Original Manuscript of the Rev. John Caspar Lavater, Citizen of Zuric* (2 vols), first published by Joseph Johnson in 1788 and reprinted in 1789 and 1794. Fuseli and

Lavater were close friends, Fuseli was working on his own book of aphorisms (not published in his lifetime), and Wollstonecraft was in process of building hers. Lavater's cover life and art, painting and poetry. An example, from his second volume, comes close to summarising one of the chief arguments of Wollstonecraft's Essay on Poetry:

> Some can be poets and painters only at second hand; deaf and blind to the tones and motions of Nature herself, they hear or see her only through some reflected medium of art; they are imboldened by prescription. (vol. ii, no. 36)

Wollstonecraft had already done some translation of Lavater (she had started a version of his *Physiognomy* in 1789, but abandoned it when Holcroft's translation appeared); but in any case Fuseli's translation, and his own composition of aphorisms, coincided with her friendship with him, and she had to be much involved in it – hence her own 'Hints'. In Fuseli's Advertisement to his translation he describes maxims as 'verdicts of wisdom on the reports of experience' (vol. i, p. v), and it is by this standard that Wollstonecraft's 'Hints' should be judged.

So far as her ideas about poetry and nature are concerned, Wollstonecraft would have found support for some of them in her wide reading. She would almost certainly have been familiar with the works of Hugh Blair, who wrote in his *Critical Dissertation on the Poems of Ossian* (London, 1763) that men in primitive societies, 'in the midst of solitary rural scenes, where the beauties of nature are their chief entertainment', are likely to write the most imaginative poetry; and that as civilisation advanced, language and style became 'more chaste; but less animated' (pp. 2, 3). The particular combination of qualities which Wollstonecraft says are necessary for the poetic character – imagination, 'faculties enlarged by thought', strong feelings – are not, however, to be found in Blair's writings, and her primary source may well have been her own experience. Godwin's description of her love of the countryside, and of her finding God there, is particularly relevant here:

> Her mind constitutionally attached itself to the sublime and the amiable. She found an inexpressible delight in the beauties of nature, and in the splendid reveries of the imagination. But nature itself, she thought, would be no better than a vast blank, if the mind of the

observer did not supply it with an animating soul.[1] When she walked amid the wonders of nature, she was accustomed to converse with her God. (Holmes (1987) p. 215)

It is also probable that some of Wollstonecraft's ideas on poetry and the imagination may have derived from – or found support in – those of Blake. She must, presumably, have known Blake for some years, since he illustrated her *Original Stories*, but she must also have known him, and his ideas, through Fuseli, with whom he became friends at the time when her own admiration for Fuseli knew no bounds. Blake's friendship with Fuseli is celebrated in the famous: 'The only man I ever knew/Who did not make me want to spew/Was Fuseli. . .', and he annotated his own copy of Fuseli's translation of Lavater's *Aphorisms* in 1788 before the book was bound (Blake (1966) p. 551, pp. 65–88). Unfortunately, there is little or no documentation of Wollstonecraft's relationship with Blake, but it is unlikely to have been less than powerful. Blake's views on poetry and the imagination are clear from his writings at this time: his *Songs of Innocence* (1789) have – to quote Gilchrist – 'that visible spontaneity, so rare and great a charm, the eloquent attribute of our old English Ballads and the early Songs of all nations' (Gilchrist (1863) vol. i, p. 7), which must recall Wollstonecraft's praise of the early poets of all nations in her essay. In addition, of course, it is well known that Blake saw God everywhere. His admiration for the old poets of a primitive tradition, and his belief in the imagination's power to transform and transcend, must have been known to Fuseli and to Wollstonecraft, which puts Wollstonecraft in the main current of Romanticism.

Wollstonecraft begins her Essay with a general observation which turns out – as is frequently the case in her writings – to be based on her own personal experience. It is fashionable, she remarks, among persons of supposedly refined taste, endlessly to praise the 'calm pleasures' of the countryside. But whenever she herself has visited the country, she has noticed how few other people are actually to be seen experiencing those beauties for themselves. This taste for the rural must, therefore, be assumed to be 'an artificial sentiment, rather inspired by poetry and romances, than a real perception of the beauties of nature' (vii, p. 7). This observation has led her to attempt to answer an important question: 'why the poetry written in the infancy of society, is most natural'. This statement may puzzle a twentieth-century reader; at the time when Wollstonecraft was writing, however, it was almost a critical commonplace – Homer's *Odyssey* and *Iliad*, for example, were viewed as primitive poetry, and admired for their naturalness and spontaneity. The Bible was also felt to contain 'sublime expression[s]' which were at the same time 'barbarous flight[s]', as Wollstonecraft puts it in 'Hints' no. 25 (v, p. 275). 'Hints' no. 24 gives another example: the oral tradition of tribal poetry – 'beautiful verses on the subjects of love and war' – produced by the Arabs in the fifth century AD (v, p. 274).

Wollstonecraft goes on to define what she means by 'natural' – this appears to be suggestive partly of an association with natural objects, and partly of immediacy or spontaneity:

> it is the transcript of immediate sensations, when fancy, awakened by the sight of interesting objects, in all their native wildness and simplicity, was most actively at work. At such moments, sensibility quickly furnishes similes, and the sublimed spirits combine with happy facility images, which bursting on him spontaneously, it is not necessary coldly to ransack the understanding or memory, till the laborious efforts of judgement exclude present sensations, and damp the fire of enthusiasm.[2]

One of the most notable features of the thinking which characterises this essay and the related passages in 'Hints' is the way in which Wollstonecraft privileges the imagination or fancy over the faculty of reason or understanding. In 'Hints' no. 24, she writes: 'The flights of imagination, and the laboured deductions of reason, appear almost incompatible' (v, p. 274). In the Essay, however, she makes an attempt to synthesise the two, or at least to indicate the reasoning faculty's contribution to the poet's character and productions. It is possible, she asserts, to discern from a poet's writings 'how far the faculties have been enlarged by thought, and stored with knowledge' (vii, p. 7): ideally, the poet must demonstrate a combination of 'profound thinking' and 'strong feelings' (vii, p. 8).

The poetic imagination is defined as the faculty which enables man to apprehend the Deity in all the external appearances of nature. Unlike the 'weak responses of ceremonial devotion', the heightened response which Wollstonecraft attributes to the poet is one of intense and apparently mystical spirituality. At these moments of 'sublime admiration . . . the world seems to contain only the mind that formed, and the mind that contemplates it'; and in the poetry which results, the poet 'speaks the language of truth and nature with resistless energy' (vii, p. 8). If the poet's reason were to be developed at the expense of his imagination, his writings might become more elegant and uniform, but this would diminish the effect of 'those involuntary sensations, which . . . are so evanescent, that they melt into new forms before they can be analyzed' (*ibid.*).

Close contact with the sublimities of nature, Wollstonecraft writes, suggested the imagery and mythology found in the writings of the ancient poets. Nothing could be more logical to a man whose primary experience is of natural objects than to imagine that the clouds could become chariots to transport a hero, or that 'an interposing deity, created by love or fear' might intervene to enable him to pass through tangled forests or across high mountains (vii, p. 8). The march of civilisation, however, has produced a progressive diminution of this spontaneous response; and the very images and language which 'now frequently appear unnatural, because they are remote' do so only because they are taken from books rather than first-hand experience and the poetic imagination it inspires (vii, pp. 8–9). In 'Hints' Wollstonecraft adds a further dimension to this question, arguing that the important quality which she calls 'individuality' is present in 'those enthusiastic flights of fancy, in which reason is left behind, without being lost sight of' ('Hints' no. 26: v, p. 275). The ancient poets, she asserts, exercised their understanding more than their imitators; but they used it to discriminate rather than to arrange (vii, p. 9).

So far, Wollstonecraft has emphasised the qualities necessary for the poet, and has been led to conclude that 'genius' is 'only another word for strong imagination' (vii, p. 9). She writes that the only poetry which is capable of 'rous[ing] the passions which amend the heart' is that which has been written as a result of contact with nature, rather than imitated from books. As she puts it in 'Hints' no. 31: '[a] writer of genius makes us feel; an inferiour author reason' (v, p. 276). This brings her back to the question she set out to answer at the beginning of the Essay: why do people respond more readily to natural descriptions in books and poetry than to nature itself? The answer seems to be that they lack the 'lively imagination' of the poet, so they require the experience to be selected, modified and concentrated by means of his enlivened imaginative faculty (vii, p. 10). People who lack a propensity for self-examination will be unable to recognise the subtle pleasures nature affords; and those who are too much concerned with appearances will never develop the ability to respond freely and spontaneously (vii, pp. 10–11).

It will be clear that the arguments of this Essay are in direct contradiction to the view expressed elsewhere in Wollstonecraft's work: that mankind is constantly moving in the direction of greater perfection. Both the poet's imagination and the reader's response are seen as being eroded by the advances of civilisation; and Wollstonecraft's ideal poet appears to be an archetypal noble savage, living in the very golden age on which she pours scorn in her other writings. In addition, the Essay places a greater emphasis on the supremacy of the imagination over the faculty of reason (or understanding) than she had allowed in her earlier work – an emphasis which immediately invites comparison with Blake's writings at this time.

That Wollstonecraft was conscious of the fact that she was contradicting her own earlier views, and made various – not entirely successful – attempts to give additional weight to the faculty of judgement, is evident both from the Essay itself and from the 'Hints'. 'Hints' no. 25, for example, which describes the first book of Genesis as 'the grand conception of an uncultivated mind', argues that the sublimity of the phrase *'Let there be light!'* could appear only to an undeveloped intellect: a more cultured mind would admire more deeply if there were evidence of a more 'comprehensive plan', and if 'wisdom was conspicuous instead of power' (v, p. 275). 'Hints' no. 28, however, takes issue with Kant's observation that the understanding is sublime and the imagination beautiful, arguing that the imagination is the faculty which enables us to respond to the sublime, and that the response is diminished in proportion as the reason is cultivated (v, p. 275). Finally, the arguments of Wollstonecraft's Essay lead her to the (problematic) conclusion that 'the sensibility must have . . . native strength' in order for modern man fully to appreciate the natural world. Thus she ends with a caveat: sensibility, which can allow such intense appreciation, can also make a man into a libertine, preferring 'the sensual tumult of love' to 'the calm pleasures of affectionate friendship' (vii, p. 11). Perhaps she was thinking of Rousseau, though she may just as easily have been remembering her own difficult relations with Fuseli or with Imlay.

Wollstonecraft's ideas on literature and creativity, both in the Essay and in 'Hints', obviously anticipate the return to nature which is fundamental to Romantic thinking. She voices a rejection of artificiality, society, and ideas drawn from the literary which reappear at their blankest in, say, Wordsworth's 'Expostulation and Reply'. As in Romanticism, there is also a renewed trust in imagination. In

Godwin's Conclusion to *Memoirs* he singles out intuition as the quality Wollstonecraft possessed and he lacked – a 'kind of witchcraft', a superior power of discrimination that enabled her to reach conclusions to which reason hardly led him (Holmes (1987) pp. 272–3). This is very much like her definition of imagination in 'Hints', where she substitutes that term for intuition: 'Reason in this world is the maker of wisdom – yet some flights of the imagination seem to reach what wisdom cannot teach' ('Hints' no. 22: v, p. 274). She is in no doubt that imagination is the basis of poetic creation: 'Poetry is the fair effervescence of the imagination and the forerunner of civilization' ('Hints' no. 23: *ibid.*), and she sees nature as the world of God which the imagination uncovers, as Wordsworth does in, for example, the climbing of Snowdon episode in the final book of *The Prelude*.

Her discussion of the relationship between contact with nature and the writing of poetry; the analysis of the qualities necessary for a poet; and the condemnation of unnatural images and diction all seem to point forward, in particular, to Wordsworth's Preface to the *Lyrical Ballads*, first published in the second edition of 1800; and to the additions in the third edition of 1802. It is tempting to suggest that Wollstonecraft's Essay was a primary influence on that much more famous Romantic document. It is certain that both Coleridge (who undoubtedly contributed much of the theory to the Preface) and Wordsworth read the Essay – either in the *Monthly Magazine* or in the revised version which Godwin published in the fourth volume of his edition of her *Posthumous Works* in 1798.

Coleridge's interest in Wollstonecraft is well documented. He had evidently read *Vindication of the Rights of Woman* early in 1796, since he adapted a quotation from it in *The Watchman* (17 March 1796). At some time in 1796 he also noted a projected (though never, apparently, accomplished) 'Epistle to Mrs Wolstoncraft [*sic*] urging her to Religion'.[3] He was still expressing a deep interest in her in January 1798 – the month in which Godwin's *Posthumous Works* appeared – according to Hazlitt's account of their first meeting. In an animated conversation over dinner, Hazlitt says, Coleridge 'dilated in a very edifying manner on Mary Wolstonecraft [*sic*] and Mackintosh', and later the same evening:

> He asked me if I had ever seen Mary Wolstonecraft, and I said, I had once for a few moments, and that she seemed to me to turn off Godwin's objections to something she advanced with quite a playful, easy air. He

replied that 'this was only one instance of the ascendency which people of imagination exercised over those of mere intellect'. (Hazlitt (1930–34) vol. xvii, pp. 111–12).

There is some evidence to suggest that Coleridge's admiration for Wollstonecraft's imagination originated – in part at least – in his reading of her *Letters Written During a Short Residence in Sweden, Norway and Denmark*; but he also had links – partly on his own account and partly through his brother-in-law and close friend Robert Southey – with the *Monthly Magazine* at this time. 'On Poetry' was published in the *Monthly Magazine* in April 1797, and an article of Southey's – one of a series on Spanish and Portuguese poetry, with original poetic translations by Southey – appears a few pages before it in the same issue as 'Continuation of Remarks on the Poetry of Spain and Portugal', signed T.Y. (*Monthly Magazine*, vol. iii, 16, pp. 270–2). In any case, the *Monthly* was taking an interest both in Wollstonecraft and in Southey and Coleridge at this time. The January 1797 issue, for instance, contains a notice of Coleridge's 'Ode to the Departed Year' and an announcement that 'A novel, entitled "The Wrongs of Woman", will shortly make its appearance, from the pen of the author of "The Rights of Woman"' (*Monthly Magazine*, vol. iii, 13, pp. 58, 59); and the same issue also contains 'Lines Addressed, from London, to SARA and S.T.C. at Bristol, in the summer of 1796', a rather graceful verse written in friendship by Charles Lamb (*ibid.*, pp. 54–5).

The May issue of the *Monthly* also had news of Coleridge's forthcoming book, 'A new edition of Mr Coleridge's Poems is in forwardness; it will contain poems by Mr Lloyd and Mr Lamb (*Monthly Magazine*, vol. iii, 17, p. 384). Southey had an article in every issue from January to April, and it seems highly probable that he would have been passing the magazine on to Coleridge, who would thus have read Wollstonecraft's Essay – Southey himself developed a profound admiration for Wollstonecraft which dates from this period, and would doubtless have drawn Coleridge's attention to the essay.[4] Since Coleridge was at this time absorbed in his friendship with Wordsworth, then, assuming that Wollstonecraft's Essay had struck a note of sympathy, he would probably have discussed it with Wordsworth. Coleridge's ability to absorb other people's views, particularly at this time, is well documented, and it has been said that the poetry he wrote in the late 1790s was influenced by

Wollstonecraft's *Letters from Sweden*,[5] so a direct influence from her Essay seems not at all unlikely. In a letter to Southey written three months after the Essay appeared in the *Monthly*, he describes Wordsworth's residence – 'All-foxen – & so divine and wild in the country that I am sure it would increase your stock of images' (Coleridge (1956–71) i, p. 366). Thus he links Wordsworth with Wollstonecraft's nature, with her early poets whose inspiration was untainted by the literary and the civilised ('wild') and whose genius is drawn directly from their experience of the wildness they inhabit.

It is probable, of course, that Wordsworth had met Wollstonecraft at Johnson's, since he was one of his authors and one of the radicals who collected around him. It is unlikely that he would not have been struck with her, as Southey and Coleridge were – they had much in common, particularly their experiences in France, where both were politically and personally involved, and both had had a child. It is known that he read Godwin's *Memoirs*, and he probably refreshed his memory of what Coleridge told him by reading or, perhaps, rereading Wollstonecraft's Essay at a time when he was putting his ideas in order preparatory to writing the 1800 Preface. Indeed, according to Duncan Wu, Wordsworth probably read the *Rights of Men* in spring 1791, the *Letters from Sweden* in 1797–8, and – more importantly – the *Monthly* from March 1797 onwards, considered writing for the magazine, and was much influenced by some of what he read in it (Wu (1993) pp. 101–3, 174). There may well have been many other influences shaping Wordsworth's ideas at this time: obviously Coleridge was a primary influence, but there were undoubtedly others, of whom Wollstonecraft must have been one. W.J.B. Owen and J.W. Smyser point to an article by William Enfield in the *Monthly* in 1796 as a possible source for the Preface (Wordsworth (1974) vol. i, p. 114), but not to Wollstonecraft's Essay, which is consistent with both Enfield and Wordsworth. It shares the primitivism of both, but the stress upon nature, imagination and the corruptions that arise from the literary and the civilised are not in Enfield's work but are in Wordsworth's, where the taste of the age is particularly condemned as artificial and gaudy.[6]

It seems certain that had she survived the birth of her daughter, Wollstonecraft might have gone on to contribute in more direct ways to the body of literature we now think of as Romantic. As it is, her thought and writings form a link – previously considered to be non-existent – between the early Romanticism of Blake and the later developments in the poetry and prose of Wordsworth and Coleridge.

◆

The Attribution of Reviews to Mary Wollstonecraft

Unfortunately, the practice of signing by letters only, together with the almost total lack of any external supporting evidence, means that it is impossible to do any more than guess at which reviews were in fact written by Wollstonecraft. Only three out of over four hundred which have been ascribed to her by various commentators are supported by external evidence.[1] Since all three of these reviews are initialled 'M', it seems reasonable to suppose that Wollstonecraft used this initial consistently. However, since she undoubtedly wrote a very large number of other reviews, commentators have also assigned to her all reviews intialled 'W', 'M.I.' (for Mary Imlay) and – more mysteriously – 'T', as well as unsigned reviews which preceded ones with these signatures. All these initials disappeared from the *Analytical* during the period (December 1792–May 1796) when Wollstonecraft was out of England. This policy has been followed by the editors of *The Works of Mary Wollstonecraft*.[2] Their policy, however, is odd, and hard to justify in so far as much that is not attributed to Wollstonecraft seems just as likely to be hers as some of that which is. For example, their attribution begins with Article xxxiii, June 1788, but Article xxx, which reviews *The History of Little Jack*, by Thomas Day, is just as likely to be by her; the book is praised for its 'practical instruction', and the notice concludes:

> Perhaps the most essential service which can be rendered to the rising generation is to make them *feel* that virtue alone is true greatness, and nature the guide to happiness.

– which could have been Wollstonecraft, and would be interesting if
it were. The same applies to Article xxxi and Article xxxii, on *Dr
Watt's Divine and Moral Songs for Children* and *Dr Watt's Hymns and
Moral Songs, for the Use of Children*, either or both of which could
have been written by Wollstonecraft. In fact the prefatory note to the
volume of her *Works* which contains the reviews states that
Wollstonecraft's 'earliest likely reviews . . . concern educational
books on algebra, grammar, history, religion and morals' (vii, p. 15),
but these prove not to have been included. The admittedly vexed
question of attribution has been discussed at length, but although the
editors say that they have 'tried to find evidence of her stylistic
characteristics and dominant opinions' before assigning reviews (vii
p. 17), they have included at least one review – of Matthew Lewis's
The Monk – which is completely different in style and content from
any of Wollstonecraft's other reviews, despite the fact that an
authoritative commentator (Derek Roper) has pointed this out at
length, and has convincingly argued that its cynical, 'man-of-the-
world' style and sentiments suggest the authorship of Fuseli (Roper
(1958) pp. 37–8). With no other evidence to go on, however, their
decisions have been accepted for the purposes of the discussion.
While it is certainly true that the major reviews do appear to carry
what are fairly conclusive hallmarks in the way of reiterated attitudes,
themes, preoccupations and even phrases, which can be found
elsewhere in Wollstonecraft's works, readers are nevertheless
cautioned to bear in mind the fact that none of these attributions (with
the exceptions already mentioned) is firm.

Notes

Chapter 1

1. Quoted in Jones (1990) p. 109.
2. For a discussion of Price's philosophy, see Thomas (1977) *passim*.
3. For discussions of *Mary* as characteristic of the genre, see, for example, Spacks (1974–5); Todd (1986).
4. Two useful and intelligent recent discussions of the subject are Myers (1986) and Briggs (1989).
5. It is interesting to note that the Kingsboroughs' elder daughter Margaret, later Lady Mount Cashell, remained a devoted disciple of her ex-governess all her life: after her elopement to Italy, where she met Wollstonecraft's daughter Mary Wollstonecraft Shelley, she adopted the name Mrs Mason and wrote educational books for women (see McAleer (1958) *passim*).

Chapter 2

1. Abinger microfilm, reel 9, Bodleian Library, Oxford.
2. Ralph Wardle's note (Wardle (1979) p. 256) that she 'first met the Christies in Paris [in 1792–3]' is obviously wrong, since she had been working under his editorship for four years.
3. See Appendix for a discussion of the vexed question of the attribution of reviews to Wollstonecraft.
4. For a discussion of the writings of Catherine Macaulay, see Hill (1992) *passim*.
5. See *The Anti-Jacobin Review*, 1 (October 1798), p. 463.
6. See Tyson (1979), pp. 135–71 for a full account of Johnson's trial and conviction.

Chapter 3

1. Burke to Unknown Correspondent, nd [1791] (Burke (1967) vi, p. 479). For a full discussion of the events surrounding the publication of *Reflections*, see Introduction, Burke (1989) pp. 1–28.
2. For arguments for the centrality of gender to Burke's pamphlet, see Paulson (1983) pp. 57–87; Furniss (1991) *passim*.
3. For a full discussion of these events, see Derry (1963) pp. 136, 150–97 and *passim*.
4. Burke's speeches were initially reproduced in the *Morning Chronicle*, although Wollstonecraft probably referred to the republished versions, which appeared in *The Parliamentary Register; or History of the Proceedings and Debates of the House of Commons* (London, 1789) vol. xxv, 1788, 1789, pp. 418–19.
5. Notes dictated to Isabella Fenwick, quoted in Wordsworth (1952–8) vol. ii, p. 476.
6. *The Gentleman's Magazine*, vol. lxi (1791) pp. 151–4.

Chapter 4

1. See, for example, Coleridge's references to the painting in a letter to Southey (11 December 1794: Coleridge (1956–71) i, p. 135); and in Coleridge (1990) p. 151 n.
2. Letter to Mrs Fuseli, quoted in Knowles (1831) i, p. 168. Knowles recounts the relationship between Fuseli and Wollstonecraft, and quotes from several of her letters (i, pp. 161–70).
3. See Perry (1986) pp. 99–119 and *passim*. For a discussion of Mary Astell's contemporaries, see Smith (1983).
4. For a discussion of patriarchal thinking during the Enlightenment, see Rendall (1985) pp. 7–32. See also Pateman (1988) *passim*.
5. See Chapter 1 on the context of *Thoughts on the Education of Daughters* for a discussion of writings on education by the bluestocking writers of the period.
6. Macaulay's *Letters on Education* is discussed in Hill (1992) pp. 158–63.
7. For a full discussion of 'Feminism and Republicanism', see Rendall (1985) pp. 33–72.
8. Quoted in Pollack (1976) p. 106.
9. *Critical Review*, 5 (1796) pp. 397, 141. For a full discussion of the reviews, see Janes (1978) pp. 293–302.

Chapter 5

1. The relationship between Helen Williams's *Letters Written in France* and the *Historical and Moral View* is discussed in Jones (1992) *passim*.
2. Priestley (1791) p. 147; Macaulay (1791) p. 20.
3. See Todd (1975) p. 11; Wardle (1951) p. 206.

4. For an intelligent discussion of the sources of Godwin's thought, see Philp (1986) pp. 15–79 (and *ibid.* pp. 175–92 for Wollstonecraft's possible influence on Godwin's changing attitudes to 'sensual commerce' and to marriage). Wollstonecraft was certainly familiar with *Political Justice* by August 1796, when she referred to it ironically in a note to Godwin (Wardle (1979) pp. 339–40). Since, however, she was by this time involved in a relationship with him, this does not help one to decide whether her renewed interest in Godwin, whom she had initially disliked, had been due to her admiration for his work, or whether she had read his work as a result of their developing relationship.

Chapter 6

1. 22 May 1795: vi, p. 406. Wollstonecraft's private letters to Imlay were published by Godwin, who destroyed the originals, in *Posthumous Works* vols iii and iv. References are to her *Works* vol. vi.
2. Wollstonecraft's first suicide attempt is not referred to in the letters extant, but her biographers have accepted Godwin's account that she 'formed a desperate purpose to die' in May 1795 (Holmes (1987) p. 248).
3. The account is given in full in Nyström (1980). See also Holmes (1987) pp. 19–26.
4. Godwin's suggestion that the work was published at the end of 1795 (Holmes (1987) p. 255) is incorrect.
5. Quoted in Parks (1964) p. 31. Translation – 'I will never forget, though I cannot well describe, this spiritual and romantic place, where the soul is elevated to a union with nature, where the huge vistas ravish the imagination, and lead to profound sentiments, to meditation on sublime objects, to an enthusiasm which makes one better and happier.'
6. Paul (1876), i, p. 228; Tomalin (1977) pp. 188–9; Wardle (1979) p. 353 n. 23; Holmes (1987) p. 279 n. 1.
7. See Myers (1979) for a similar argument which comes, however, to rather different conclusions.
8. See James Thomson, *The Seasons* (1727) and Mark Akenside, *The Pleasures of Imagination* (1744).
9. See, for example, Wordsworth (1985) pp. 3, 25, 98.
10. See also her Essay on Poetry (discussed in Chapter 8) for a development of these ideas.

Chapter 7

1. Compare Wollstonecraft's remarks on prostitution in the *Rights of Woman* and her review of *The Evils of Adultery and Prostitution* (*Analytical Review*, 14, September 1792: vii, pp. 457–9).
2. For a useful discussion of conditions in hospitals during this period, see Langford (1989) pp. 134–41.

Chapter 8

1. It is difficult not to be reminded of Shelley – Wollstonecraft's daughter's husband – who wrote in 'Mont Blanc': 'But what were thou, and earth, and stars, and sea,/If to the human mind's imaginings/Silence and solitude were vacancy?' (ll.142–4).
2. Quoted from the original version of the essay, as it appeared in *The Monthly Magazine*. It is interesting to compare this version with the one published by Godwin (vii, pp. 7–11), who, among other substantial changes, removed or amended no fewer than four references to the imagination as well as 'bursting on him spontaneously' in the passage quoted here.
3. Coleridge (1957) Note 261. Kathleen Coburn suggests that the favourable review of *Letters Written . . . in Sweden* in the *Critical Review* of February 1796 (vol. vii, pp. 602–10) may have been written by Coleridge.
4. See Jump (1992).
5. The suggestion was first made by John Livingston Lowes (1951) p. 593 n. 27. See also Holmes (1987) pp. 39–40.
6. For an argument suggesting that several of the poems in Wordsworth's *Lyrical Ballads* were also influenced by his reading of Godwin's *Memoirs* and Wollstonecraft's *Posthumous Works*, see Jump (1992).

Appendix

1. One review, of *A Sermon written by the late Samuel Johnson, LLD for the Funeral of his Wife*, is mentioned in a letter of 1788 (Wardle (1979) p. 179); a letter to Godwin in 1797 asks him to return Ann Radcliffe's *The Italian* 'because I promised to let Johnson have it this week' (Wardle (1979) p. 384); and the draft of one review, of the novel *Albert de Nordenschild*, exists in holograph manuscript.
2. See 'Prefatory Note' (vii, pp. 14–18) for a discussion of the editorial policy.

References

All references to Mary Wollstonecraft's works within the text, unless otherwise stated, are taken from Marilyn Butler and Janet Todd (eds) (1989) *The Works of Mary Wollstonecraft*, 7 vols, Pickering & Chatto, London.

I. Contemporary British periodicals

The Analytical Review, or History of Literature, Domestic and Foreign
The Annual Register
The Anti-Jacobin Review
The British Critic
The Critical Review: or Annals of Literature
The Monthly Magazine
The Monthly Review or Literary Journal
The New Annual Register

II. Books and articles

Althusser, Louis (1984) 'Ideology and Ideological State Apparatuses', in *Essays on Ideology*, Verso, London, pp. 1–60.

Blake, William (1966) *The Complete Writings*, ed. Geoffrey Keynes, Oxford University Press, London.

Briggs, Julia (1989) 'Women Writers and Writing for Children: From Sarah Fielding to E. Nesbit', in G. Avery and J. Briggs (eds), *Children and their Books: A Celebration of the Work of Iona and Peter Opie*, Clarendon Press, Oxford, pp. 221–50.

Burke, Edmund (1967) *The Correspondence vol. iv, July 1789–Dec 1791*, eds Alfred Cobban and Robert A. Smith, Cambridge University Press, Cambridge.

Burke, Edmund (1987) *A Philosophical Enquiry into the Origin of our Ideas of the Sublime and Beautiful*, ed. James T. Boulton, Blackwell, Oxford.

Burke, Edmund (1989) *Writings and Speeches*, vol. viii, *The French Revolution 1790–1794*, ed. L.G. Mitchell, Clarendon Press, Oxford.

Coleridge, Samuel Taylor (1956–71) *Collected Letters*, ed. E.L. Griggs, 6 vols, Clarendon Press, Oxford.

Coleridge, Samuel Taylor (1957) *Notebooks*, ed. Kathleen Coburn, vol. i (1794–1804), Bollingen Series L, Pantheon Books, New York.

Coleridge, Samuel Taylor (1990) *Table Talk, Collected Works of Samuel Taylor Coleridge*, Bollingen Series LXXV, Princeton University Press, Princeton, NJ.

Cunningham, Allan (1879) 'Life of Fuseli', in *Lives of the Most Eminent British Painters*, ed. C. Heaton, 3 vols, George Bell & Son, London, vol. ii, pp. 40–101.

Derry, J.W. (1963) *The Regency Crisis and the Whigs, 1788–9*, Cambridge University Press, Cambridge.

Dowden, Edward (1897) *The French Revolution and English Literature*, Kegan Paul & Co, London.

Furniss, Tom (1991) 'Gender & Revolution: Edmund Burke and Mary Wollstonecraft', in Kelvin Everest (ed.), *Revolution in Writing: British Literary Responses to the French Revolution*, Open University Press, Milton Keynes, pp. 65–100.

Gaunt, William (1956) *Arrows of Desire: A Study of William Blake and his Romantic World*, Museum Press, London.

Gilchrist, W. (1863) *Life of William Blake*, 2 vols, Macmillan, London and Cambridge.

Godwin, William (1793) *An Enquiry Concerning Political Justice and its Influence on Virtue and Happiness*, 2 vols, Robinson, London.

Hazlitt, William (1930–34) *The Complete Works*, ed. P.P. Howe, 21 vols, Dent, London and Toronto.

Hill, Bridget (1992) *The Republican Virago: The Life and Times of Catherine Macaulay*, Clarendon Press, Oxford.

Holmes, Richard (ed.) (1987) Mary Wollstonecraft, *A Short Residence in Sweden, Norway and Denmark* and William Godwin, *Memoirs of the Author of the Rights of Woman*, Penguin, Harmondsworth.

Janes, R.N. (1978) 'On the Reception of Mary Wollstonecraft's *A Vindication of the Rights of Woman*', *Journal of the History of Ideas* 39, 1, 293–302.

Jones, Vivien (ed.) (1990) *Women in the Eighteenth Century: Constructions of Femininity*, Routledge, London and New York.

Jones, Vivien (1992) 'Women Writing Revolution: Narratives of History and Sexuality in Wollstonecraft and Williams', in Stephen Copley and John Whale (eds), *Beyond Romanticism: New Approaches to Texts and Contexts 1780–1832*, Routledge, London and New York, pp. 178–99.

Jump, Harriet Devine (1992) 'No Equal Mind: Mary Wollstonecraft and the Young Romantics', *Charles Lamb Bulletin*, New Series, 79 (July), 225–38.

Kaplan, Cora (1986) 'Wild Nights: Pleasure/Sexuality/Feminism', republished in *Sea Changes: Culture and Feminism*, Verso, London, pp. 31–56.

Kelly, Gary (1989) *English Fiction of the Romantic Period 1789–1830*, Longman, London and New York.

Kelly, Gary (1992) *Revolutionary Feminism: The Mind and Career of Mary Wollstonecraft*, Macmillan, London.

Knowles, John (1831) *The Life and Writings of Henry Fuseli, Esq, M.A.F.A.*, 3 vols, Henry Colburn and Richard Bentley, London.

Langford, Paul (1989) *A Polite and Commercial People: England 1727–1783*, Oxford University Press, Oxford.

Lorch, Jennifer (1990) *Mary Wollstonecraft: The Making of a Radical Feminist*, Berg Press, New York, Oxford and Munich.

Lowes, John Livingstone (1951) *The Road to Xanadu: A Study in the Ways of the Imagination*, Constable, London, 1927, 2nd rev. edn 1951.

McAleer, E.C. (1958) *The Sensitive Plant: A Life of Lady Mount Cashell*, University of North Carolina Press, Chapel Hill.

Macaulay, Catherine (1790) *Letters on Education. With Observations on Religious and Metaphysical Subjects*, Dilly, London.

Macaulay, Catherine (1791) *Observations on the Reflections of the Right Hon. Edmund Burke . . . In a Letter to the Right Hon. Earl of Stanhope*, Dilly, London.

Moore, Jane (1992) 'Plagiarism with a Difference: Subjectivity in "Kubla Khan" and *Letters Written During a Short Residence in Sweden, Norway and Denmark*', in Stephen Copley and John Whale (eds), *Beyond Romanticism: New Approaches to Texts and Contexts 1780–1832*, Routledge, London and New York, pp. 140–59.

Myers, Mitzi (1979) 'Mary Wollstonecraft's *Letters Written . . . in Sweden*: Towards Romantic Autobiography', *Studies in Eighteenth-Century Culture*, 8, 165–85.

Myers, Mitzi (1986) 'Impeccable Governesses, Rational Dames, and Moral Mothers: Mary Wollstonecraft and the Female Tradition in Georgian Children's Books', *Children's Literature*, vol. 14, Yale University Press, New Haven, CT and London, 31–59.

Nichols, John (1812–1815) *Literary Anecdotes of the Eighteenth Century*, 9 vols, Nichols, Son & Bentley, London.

Nyström, Per (1980) *Mary Wollstonecraft's Scandinavian Journey*, RSAS Gothenburg, *Humaniora* 17.

Parks, George B. (1964) 'The Turn to the Romantic in the Travel Literature of the Eighteenth Century', *Modern Language Quarterly* 25, 22–33.

Pateman, Carole (1988) *The Sexual Contract*, Polity Press, Cambridge.

Paul, Charles Kegan (1876) *William Godwin, His Friends and Contemporaries*, 2 vols, King & Co., London.

Paulson, Ronald (1983) 'Burke, Paine and Wollstonecraft: The Sublime and the Beautiful', in *Representations of Revolution (1789–1820)*, Yale University Press, New Haven, CT and London.

Perry, Ruth (1986) *The Celebrated Mary Astell: An Early English Feminist*, University of Chicago Press, Chicago and London.

Philp, M. (1986) *Godwin's Political Justice*, Duckworth, London.

Pollack, John (1976) *Wilberforce*, Lion, Tring.

Poovey, Mary (1984) *The Proper Lady and the Woman Writer: Ideology as Style in the Works of Mary Wollstonecraft, Mary Shelley and Jane Austen,* University of Chicago Press, Chicago and London.

Price, Richard (1789) *A Discourse on the Love of our Country,* Cadell, London.

Priestley, Joseph (1791) *Letter to the Right Honourable Edmund Burke, Occasioned by his Reflections on the Revolution in France,* T. Pearson, Birmingham.

Reiss, Timothy (1989) 'Revolution in Bounds: Wollstonecraft, Women, and Reason', in Linda Kauffman (ed.), *Gender and Theory: Dialogues on Feminist Criticism,* Blackwell, Oxford.

Rendall, Jane (1985) *The Origins of Modern Feminism: Women in Britain, France and the United States, 1780–1860,* Macmillan, Basingstoke and London.

Rickman, Thomas C. (1819) *The Life of Thomas Paine,* Rickman & Son, London.

Roper, Derek (1958) 'Mary Wollstonecraft's Reviews', *Notes and Queries* 203, 37–8.

Rousseau, Jean-Jacques (1974) *Émile,* trans. Barbara Foxley, Dent, London.

Schama, Simon (1989) *Citizens: A Chronicle of the French Revolution,* Penguin, Harmondsworth.

Smith, Hilda L. (1983) *Reason's Disciples: Seventeenth-Century English Feminists,* University of Illinois Press, Urbana, Chicago and London.

Spacks, P.M. (1974–5) 'Every Woman is at Heart a Rake', *Eighteenth-Century Studies,* 27–46.

Spacks, P.M. (1976) *Imagining a Self: Autobiography and Novel in Eighteenth-Century England,* Harvard University Press, Cambridge, MA.

St Clair, William (1989) *The Godwins and the Shelleys: The Biography of a Family,* Faber & Faber, London.

Sullivan, Alvin (ed.) (1983) *British Literary Magazines: The Romantic Age 1789–1836,* Greenwood, New York and London.

Thomas, D.O. (1977) *The Honest Mind: The Thought and Work of Richard Price,* Clarendon Press, Oxford.

Todd, Janet M. (ed.) (1975) *Mary Wollstonecraft: An Historical and Moral View,* Scholars' Facsimiles and Reprints, Garland, New York and London.

Todd, Janet M. (ed.) (1976) *Mary Wollstonecraft: An Annotated Bibliography,* Garland, New York and London.

Todd, Janet M. (1980) *Women's Friendship in Literature,* Columbia University Press, New York.

Todd, Janet M. (1986) *Sensibility: An Introduction,* Methuen, London.

Todd, Janet M. (1990) *A Wollstonecraft Anthology,* Polity Press, Cambridge.

Tomalin, Claire (1977) *The Life and Death of Mary Wollstonecraft,* Penguin, Harmondsworth.

Tyson, Gerald P. (1979) *Joseph Johnson: A Liberal Publisher,* University of Iowa Press, Iowa City.

Wardle, Ralph M. (1951) *Mary Wollstonecraft: A Critical Biography,* Richards Press, London.

Wardle, Ralph M. (1979) *Collected Letters of Mary Wollstonecraft,* Cornell University Press, Ithaca, NY and London.

Williams, Helen Maria (1790) *Letters Written in France, in the Summer of 1790 to a Friend in England*, vol. i, T. Cadell, London.

Williams, Helen Maria (1793) *Letters from France*, vols iii and iv, G.G. and J. Robinson, London.

Wilson, Ellen Gibson (1989) *Thomas Clarkson: A Biography*, Macmillan, London.

Wordsworth, William (1952–8) *The Poetical Works*, eds E. de Selincourt and H. Darbishire, 5 vols, 1940–49; 2nd edn, vols 1–4, rev. H. Darbishire, Clarendon Press, Oxford.

Wordsworth, William (1967) *The Letters of William and Dorothy Wordsworth*, ed. E. de Selincourt; *The Early Years, 1787–1805*, rev. C.L. Shaver, Clarendon Press, Oxford.

Wordsworth, William (1974) *The Prose Works*, eds W.J.B. Owen and J.W. Smyser, 3 vols, Clarendon Press, Oxford.

Wordsworth, William (1985) *The Prelude 1799, 1805, 1850*, eds Jonathan Wordsworth, M.H. Abrams and Stephen Gill, Norton, New York and London.

Wordsworth, William and Coleridge, Samuel Taylor (1991) *Lyrical Ballads*, ed. R.L. Brett and A.R. Jones, Methuen, London and New York, 1963; rev. 1991.

Wu, Duncan (1993) *Wordsworth's Reading 1770–1799*, Cambridge University Press, Cambridge.

Yaeger, Patricia (1989) 'Towards a Female Sublime', in Linda Kauffman (ed.), *Gender and Theory: Dialogues on Feminist Criticism*, Blackwell, Oxford, pp. 191–212.

Young, Arthur (1792) *Travels During the Years 1787, 1788 and 1789*, J. Rackham, Bury St Edmunds.

Young, Arthur (1793) *The Example of France a Warning to Britain*, M. Richardson, London.

Further Reading

Abrams, M.H. (1969) *The Mirror and the Lamp: Romantic Theory and Critical Tradition*, Norton, New York.

Ackland, Michael (1982–3) 'The Embattled Sexes: Blake's Debt to Wollstonecraft in The Four Zoas', *Blake* 16 (Winter), 172–83.

Alexander, Meena (1989) *Women in Romanticism: Mary Wollstonecraft, Dorothy Wordsworth and Mary Shelley*, Macmillan, London.

Barker-Benfield, G.J. (1989) 'Mary Wollstonecraft: Eighteenth-Century Commonwealth-woman', *Journal of the History of Ideas* 50, 95–115.

Boulton, James T. (1963) *The Language of Politics in the Age of Wilkes and Burke*, Routledge & Kegan Paul, London; and University of Toronto Press, Toronto.

Brody, Miriam (1983) 'Mary Wollstonecraft: Sexuality and Women's Rights', in Dale Spender (ed.), *Feminist Theorists*, The Women's Press, London, pp. 40–59.

Butler, Marilyn (ed.) (1984) *Burke, Paine, Godwin, and the Revolution Controversy*, Cambridge University Press, Cambridge.

Cameron, K.N. (1961) *Shelley and His Circle, 1773–1822*, Harvard University Press, Cambridge, MA; and Oxford University Press, London.

Garrett, C. (1975) *Respectable Folly: Millenarians and the French Revolution in France and England*, Johns Hopkins University Press, Baltimore, MD and London.

Godwin, William (1992) *The Collected Novels and Memoirs*, General Editor Mark Philip, 8 vols, Pickering and Chatto, London.

Goodwin, A. (1979) *The Friends of Liberty: The English Democratic Movement in the Age of the French Revolution*, Hutchinson, London.

Jacobus, Mary (1979) 'The Difference of View', in M. Jacobus (ed.), *Women Writing and Writing about Women*, Croom Helm with Oxford University Women's Studies Committee, London; and Barnes & Noble, New York, pp. 10–21.

Kaplan, Cora (1985) 'Pandora's Box: Subjectivity, Class and Sexuality in Socialist Feminist Criticism', in G. Greene and C. Khan (eds), *Making a Difference: Feminist Literary Criticism*, Methuen, London and New York, pp. 146–76.

Myers, Mitzi (1977) 'Politics from the Outside: Mary Wollstonecraft's First *Vindication*', *Studies in Eighteenth-Century Culture*, 6, 113–32.

Myers, Mitzi (1980) 'Unfinished Business: Wollstonecraft's *Maria*', *Wordsworth Circle* 11, 2, 107–14.

Myers, Mitzi (1981) 'Godwin's *Memoirs* of Wollstonecraft: The Shaping of Self and Subject', *Studies in Romanticism*, 20, 299–316.

Myers, Mitzi (1982) 'Reform or Ruin: "A Revolution in Female Manners"', *Studies in Eighteenth-Century Culture*, 11, 199–216.

Myers, Mitzi (1988) 'Pedagogy as Self-Expression in Mary Wollstonecraft: Exorcising the Past, Finding a Voice', in Shari Benstock (ed.), *The Private Self: Theory and Practice of Women's Autobiographical Writings*, University of North Carolina Press, Chapel Hill and London, pp. 192–210.

Myers, Mitzi (1990) 'Sensibility and the "Walk of Reason": Mary Wollstonecraft's Literary Reviews as Cultural Critique', in S. McMillen Conger (ed.), *Sensibility in Transformation: Creative Resistance to Sentiment from the Augustans to the Romantics: Essays in Honor of Jean H. Hagstrum*, Farleigh Dickinson University Press, Rutherford, NJ; and Associated University Presses, London, pp. 120–44.

Myers, Sylvia Harcstark (1990) *The Bluestocking Circle: Women, Friendship, and the Life of the Mind in Eighteenth-Century England*, Clarendon Press, Oxford.

Rajan, Tillotama (1988) 'Wollstonecraft and Godwin: Reading the Secrets of the Political Novel', *Studies in Romanticism*, 27, 221–51.

Rogers, Katherine M. (1982) *Feminism in Eighteenth-Century England*, Harvester Wheatsheaf, Hemel Hempstead.

Roper, Derek (1978) *Reviewing before the Edinburgh 1788–1802*, University of Delaware Press, Newark, NJ.

Sargent, Linda (ed.) (1991) *The Unhappy Marriage of Marxism and Feminism: A Debate on Class and Patriarchy*, Pluto, London.

Spencer, Jane (1986) *The Rise of the Woman Novelist from Aphra Behn to Jane Austen*, Blackwell, Oxford.

Vickery, Alice Drysdale [1912] *The First Essay on the Political Rights of Woman. A Translation of Condorcet's Essay 'Sur l'admission des femmes au droit de cité'*, Garden City Press, Letchworth, Herts.

Index